Christian Courtship

IN AN

OverSexed World

Christian Courtship

IN AN

Over Sexed World

A Guide
for
Catholics

T. G. Morrow

Our Sunday Visitor Publishing Division
Our Sunday Visitor, Inc.
Huntington, Indiana 46750

Our Sunday Visitor Publishing Division
Our Sunday Visitor, Inc.
200 Noll Plaza
Huntington, IN 46750

ISBN: 978-1-931709-56-9 (Inventory No. T33)
LCCN: 2003105344

Cover design by Troy Lefevra
Interior design by Robert L. Hoffman

PRINTED IN THE UNITED STATES OF AMERICA

I wish to thank very much those who helped me in this endeavor: first, Barbara Meng, who so diligently read every word herein and made innumerable corrections; and my theological mentor, Dr. William May, for reading the two chapters on marriage and suggesting improvements; and Mike Aquilina, for so kindly publishing my column on courtship in *New Covenant* Magazine, and for suggesting I write a book on this. Sincere thanks also to Pete and Barbara DiGioia and their family for allowing me to use their house at the beach to do much of the writing herein; and to Susan Bucheit, Maribeth Harper, Susan Gray, Dori Belmont, and Christine Creech for reviewing several chapters and making recommendations. I am also grateful to Luis Brown and Carolyn Pierce for their contributions, and to Susan Mea.

Note: The names and some incidental circumstances have been changed in the true stories herein to protect the privacy of those involved.

Table of Contents

Introduction

Courtship: the pursuing of an intimate friendship to see if marriage would be desirable.

The typical scenario in the United States is for a couple to meet, to start dating seriously two or three times a week or more, to sleep together after the third date, and to get married after about a year and a half. What follows is a 50 percent chance of divorce (unless they live together before marriage, in which case the chances of divorce are 74 percent). This is not to mention the high rate of venereal disease (according to the Centers for Disease Control and Prevention, 65 million people in the U.S. have an incurable sexually transmitted disease) as well the bad treatment of women both before and during marriage.

If you're satisfied with all of that, I don't think you'll like this book. But, if you think things have gone awry in the last forty years, that the dating scene is a bit bizarre, and that we need to start over to build a new system for courtship, this book may be just what you are looking for.

If you think we might find some remedies for the sadness we have wrought, by looking to Jesus Christ and his Church, read on. However, I must warn you, what's written here is a bit radical, perhaps as radical as the Gospel itself. This book is for those who want to do things the way Jesus would do them, which is a truly radical thing (and always has been). Nonetheless, I am certain that if you carry out what's written here you will be happy in this life, and in the next.

A Priest Speaks on Courtship?

We had been going together for almost a year — virtually since we had met. She had blue-black hair with dark Irish eyes and was bright, and religious with a sparkling personality. Let's call her Judy McIntyre. We had often talked about the possibility of marriage, so what I said to her that day must have come as a surprise.

"Judy," I said, "There's no point in our continuing this relationship."

"Why not?" Her disappointment was evident.

"Because I'm going to become a priest."

Thus ended my first great romance at age six. I was sure God wanted me to become a priest. Judy and I were both first-graders at St. Gabriel's School in Riverdale, New York, and, as I look back, rather precocious.

I continued in that mind set for the next nine years, opting to study Latin in my freshman and sophomore years of high school to prepare for my vocation to the priesthood. Then, I discovered girls. I toyed with the idea of marrying and then becoming an Eastern Rite priest, but, in time I gave up on priesthood altogether.

So, although I had casually dated on and off through junior high and early high school, in sophomore year I began to go out more, with the prospect of marriage in the back of my mind. I had my first great love in college (or second, with due respect to Judy). She was a California blonde with a delightful personality and was Catholic, but only marginally. After we had dated for several months, she fell for another student, whom she eventually married.

Then there was Sallye in Los Angeles, where I had gone to work as an engineer after college. Another blonde, she had the added appeal of being a devout Catholic. Things began swimmingly, but after a few months she opted for a pen pal who came back from his army assignment and swept her off her feet.

Finally there was Mary, from Belmont, Massachusetts, whom I met while employed outside of Boston. She was from a delightful, devout Catholic family and was devout herself. When she answered my proposal with "Probably," I had great hope since my own mother had responded thus to my father when he proposed. However, Mary's "probably" was not as firm as my mother's. Mary eventually married her previous sweetheart, much to my sorrow.

Through the years of dating from the age of 18 or so until I was 33, I tried to live chastely and while I dated some Catholics, I mostly dated non-Catholics, foolishly hoping that we could work out our religious differences before marrying. During this time I was saddened by the fact that there seemed to be so few groups in the Church where one could go to meet a good, lively Catholic woman. I remember thinking that if I ever got the chance I would try to do something to provide help for single Catholics to live chastely and find others who wanted to do the same. (How I would do that as a married man was quite a mystery.)

At the age of 31 I began to pray in earnest for my vocation. Instead of praying one Rosary a day, which I had done since the age of 14, I began to pray two a day. I kept asking what the Lord wanted me to do with my life and promising that I would do whatever he wanted. At the age of 33, just under a year after Mary and I had parted ways, I felt a strong call to the priesthood. All my hopes and plans for marriage quickly faded as I felt a powerful happiness come over me when I resolved to accept God's call.

I entered St. Charles Seminary in Philadelphia in 1977 and was ordained for the Archdiocese of Washington (DC) in 1982. In my various parish assignments I became chaplain to our young adults groups, but all seemed quite unsuccessful in attracting good numbers of vibrant Catholic men and women. When I was moved to St. Matthew's Cathedral in 1991, I encountered another such young adults group: small and quiet.

One evening, as we discussed upcoming plans, I suggested that if we were to hold a workshop on "Christian Dating in An Oversexed World," we could probably draw sixty people. I had noticed that many young adults were coming for prayer and confessions as well as daily and Sunday Mass. It seemed certain that if we came up with a good program we could draw a large number of young people. The eight or so members at the meeting responded enthusiastically to my proposal.

We put together a program based on the Scriptures, the Church's 1975 Declaration on sexual ethics, C. S. Lewis' *The Four Loves*, and Pope John Paul II's *Love and Responsibility*. We made up some fliers with a picture of a happy-looking couple, and got them into every parish we could think of. The program was to take place on three consecutive Friday nights, right after work, with pizza at the break.

It was a smashing success. We followed up the next fall with a monthly talk on the faith, and a repeat of the dating series in a larger hall, which drew 115 each week. We held the same seminar three more times over the years, always with good attendance and receptive participants.

I must say all this surprised me. Many people are shy about mentioning chastity to single adults, thinking they won't buy it or that it might turn them away. But, in fact, these young people were delighted to hear someone speak about it, and they wanted to meet others who were there to hear about it.

At both seminar series, I mentioned the possibility of single-sex groups. I remarked that when I was a young bachelor in Los Angeles I was invited on a blind date to a "Spinsters" dance. These women, who were anything *but* spinsters, had organized their own group to create their own kind of social life.

There were no takers for the single-sex idea. However, several months later I mentioned the idea to two young women who had come to see me for spiritual guidance, and they decided to go for it. The St. Catherine Society — in honor of the patroness of single women, St. Catherine of Alexandria — was born a few weeks later. I approached every young devout woman I saw at Mass or at our monthly talks, to invite her to consider joining the group. By the time the first meeting was held, about ten women attended. We met monthly for the Rosary, dinner, and discussion of a religious topic.

It quickly became clear that the women wanted a group where they could support each other in living the Catholic faith, and learn more about the faith as well. I had to do much of the recruiting since I was the one who saw scores of new people each month, but the rate of commitment was over 50 percent for those who came even once.

These women were dedicated to, as their promotional card indicated, "Daily prayer, especially the Rosary, weekday Mass when feasible, spiritual reading, living a moral life, and Christian hospitality and service." After a few years nearly three-quarters of them were going to daily Mass, praying the Rosary daily, and reading spiritual books. And, once they got going, they came up with all sorts of solid spiritual activities, and social activities with a spiritual theme as well.

Three years later, the men formed a counterpart group — the St. Lawrence Society. I think the hope of mixing socially from time to time with the St. Catherine Society was a huge factor in motivating the men to finally come together. They too became very active in the faith. They established their own lecture series on the faith, bringing in speakers such as Father Benedict Groeschel and Father Peter Stravinskas, and Mary Beth Bonacci, a chastity expert.

On the subject of chastity, early on, unbeknown to me, two of our St. Catherine's members worried that because I insisted on including chastity as part of the program, they weren't sure it would work because it was difficult to find men who would go along with it.

A year later, they told me about this conversation, and laughed at their skepticism. It had worked. In fact, if we hadn't included chastity, the whole project would have failed. The gospel has never worked at anything less than 100 percent.

One of these same women told me later, "Father, I always wanted to live this way, but I never knew how. This is the happiest time of my life."

Much more will be said of the St. Catherine and St. Lawrence Societies in a later chapter, but to return to the original question: Why is a *priest* writing about Christian courtship?

First, as one who dated for eleven years after college, I have experienced the difficulties of trying to remain a Christian in our oversexed world. Second, many have asked me to write about the "Christian Dating" seminars we held in Washington. Third, having worked closely with our young adults in the St. Catherine and St. Lawrence Societies since 1992, I know Christian courtship is possible and worth every bit of the effort. It's been a delight to see how these wonderful Catholics, many of whom have become my dear friends, have succeeded in living out the faith and marrying well. Finally, I resolved before entering the seminary to work to help young single Catholics to survive the post-sexual-revolution "dating scene." That's why I wanted to write this book.

So, here goes.

Chapter One

Choosing Mr./Miss Right

It is surprising how many young men and women have barely a clue as to what to look for in a potential spouse. Most simply try to find someone they are attracted to and then fall into a relationship. If there are no major crises along the way, or even if there are, they get married and hope it works.

There is a better way: Establish what you should be looking for before you get started.

Consider Your Salvation

The first consideration in choosing a spouse is, "Will this person help me to get to God's Kingdom?" For any good Catholic, salvation should be the prime consideration in any endeavor.

What kind of person *will* help you to be saved? In this day and age, from what I've observed, your best choice by far is a solid, practicing Catholic. Why? Because of our current moral crisis. Look realistically at the issues facing couples nowadays: sexual activity during courtship; abortion and contraception (much of which is abortifacient); the number of children (good Catholics tend to be open to having more than the average number); Sunday worship;

baptizing and educating children in the Faith; schooling, includ-ing the choice of Catholic, secular or home; etc. The list seems to grow by the hour.

You will share your whole life in the most intimate of relation-ships with the person you marry. No person on earth will be closer to you, not even your father or mother. (See Genesis 2:24.) Do you really want to spend a good deal of time in your marriage arguing with a spouse who will fight you on contraception, or going to Sun-day Mass; or who won't give you an ounce of support in your most important lifelong mission? Wouldn't you rather have someone who will actually support you rather than fight you? Salvation is hard enough without having to drag an unwilling spouse along behind you!

Is there any possibility for a relationship with a non-Catholic? Perhaps, but these moral issues can be difficult for Catholics, not to mention non-Catholics. The question to ask is if he/she is open to your moral convictions. Chances are, only a devout Protestant who sees the goodness of the Catholic faith would be.

What if you meet a lapsed Catholic or an atheist who seems very nice? My advice has always been that if they don't become more religious during the first six months of the courtship, there's a good chance they will never accept Christ or the Church. If you marry this person, you may well find that your most intimate friend on this earth will in no way help you on your journey toward the Kingdom.

But isn't that journey ultimately our own responsibility? Sure. But when you go about attaining an objective, from winning a base-ball game to securing a contract, don't you want to have every-thing in your favor? Why tie one hand behind your back when you pursue the ultimate goal, eternal life?

Now some might say, "Well, Father, that's easy for you to say, but it's hard to find someone you like. If you add these sorts of conditions, it will be next to impossible!"

I agree it will certainly narrow the field. But remember, God doesn't say "I call you to the vocation of marriage. Now go find someone on your own." God is there to help. If you say, "Lord, I'm going to seek someone who loves you so we can nourish each other in that love," do you think God will say, "Good luck!" I think he will rather say, "Great. I'll help you find someone."

Many other elements go into choosing a marriage partner, but if you get this one wrong, you could be in for a lifetime of deep trouble.

How do you know if someone is a good Catholic? One thing you *don't* do is to ask. Virtually everyone thinks he/she is a good Catholic or Christian even if he/she hasn't set foot in a church or prayed in years. Observe! Does he/she go to Mass each Sunday? Does he/she go to confession? Is he/she willing to live gospel chastity, not just for you but for Christ? Does he/she pray regularly? Is he/she willing to pray with you? Can he/she talk about these things? Often if the person refuses to talk about his/her own spirituality, it's because he/she doesn't have much of it. If you're considering marrying someone, you have every right to know how he/she relates to your best friend, God. Is he/she willing to learn more about the Faith by reading, etc.? Does he/she understand the Cross, i.e., that following Christ and loving others is hard, and involves real sacrifice? (This is a big one.)

You need not quiz someone on the first date, but as the relationship develops, you should indicate little things about your own spiritual life and see how he/she responds. If you never get a response, you might have to be more direct: "Would you like to pray together some time?" If he/she responds, "That's kind of personal," you could counter, "Yes, I'm looking for a personal relationship." After all, what could be more personal than marriage?

Don't sell yourself short. I have worked with lots of young, single Catholics who found good, religious spouses, people who share their own values. You don't have to compromise in this area, unless you give up before you start, as so many do. It takes some planning and effort to find a religious mate, but it is quite possible, and definitely worth it.

The Desire for Children

Next, does he/she like children? Does he/she want a generous sized family? Or, does he/she want to limit the number of children for selfish motives or out of fear? The Church has high praise for those who "with wise and common deliberation" are generous enough to bring up "suitably" a large number of children.[1]

Does he/she want to dedicate time to raising children? Does he/she believe in having a mother at home for children, and a father who supports them? Can this person be patient with children? Anyone who has children has got to be flexible, and to roll with the punches.

Is he/she responsible? Can he/she be firm yet gentle? Some of these things may be hard to discover, but if you and your sweetheart spend some time around children — nephews or nieces or children of friends — you can observe his/her behavior then. It's not necessary that he/she be a child psychologist, but he/she should be very interested in raising children with character and be willing to learn how to do that.

Evaluate Communication

Is this person a good communicator? The key here, of course, is whether or not they can diplomatically let you know that they are not happy with your behavior. For example, "You slob, you left your clothes on the floor again," just won't cut it in a good marriage. But, "Darling, you know how much I love and appreciate everything you do for me. I wonder if you could add just one little thing? Could you just try to put your dirty clothes in the hamper, please?"

This ability to honor your spouse when you try to correct him/her is a major issue in marriage. The trick is to be able to express your desires in a positive way, without nagging. We'll talk more about this in the chapter on communication.

Red Lights and Warning Signs

Does he/she have any major hang-ups, such as being a drug user or dealer, an unreformed alcoholic, or a compulsive gambler? Any of these should set off red lights everywhere. Marrying someone like this is an invitation to disaster. If you are frequently attracted to such people, get counseling right away!

One lovely young woman came to me and asked what she should do about her boyfriend, who took and even sold drugs. I told her, "Get rid of him today! He's trouble!"

"But I love him," she insisted.

"Love won't conquer a drug habit. Don't make yourself miserable for years and years for a few moments of pleasure." I never heard what she did. I hope she got smart.

Once a woman asked me what I thought about her continuing with her boyfriend. "He prays the Rosary, and goes to Mass often during the week. But, well, he's trying to get me into kinky sex."

"Run for the hills, I told her. This guy is a terrible hypocrite." (She needed *me* to tell her this?)

Another danger: Does he/she have a lot of unresolved anger? Anger is poison to a marriage. If someone is angry a good deal of the time, he or she needs to resolve this through therapy before marriage. Otherwise, they're going to be big trouble to any prospective spouse.

A husband once told me his wife would get angry with him and refuse to talk to him for two weeks at a time. What infantile behavior! When you're angry with your sweetheart, you may need some time to cool off, but after that you need to be able to talk. Silence as a weapon is utter folly.

To the person who says, "But I can change him (or her)," I say, "Go into religious life. Then you can reform people without having to live with them." Gandhi was right on the mark when he said, "A reformer cannot afford to have close intimacy with him whom he seeks to reform."

The Freedom to Marry

Another thing to be careful about is making sure the person you meet is free to marry. If you find out this person was married before, the first question to ask is "Do you have an annulment?" If their previous marriage was outside the Church, and either they or their spouse was a Catholic, their marriage was invalid, and getting an annulment is little more than a formality. If, however, they were married in the Church, or neither one was Catholic, they would need to get an annulment before they would be free to marry. (A non-Catholic can get an annulment in the Catholic Church if he/she would like to marry a Catholic.)

So what if you ask if he/she has an annulment and the answer is no? I recommend you simply say, "If you get an annulment, let me know. Then perhaps we can get together again if you like." Some people have no intention of getting an annulment, yet, they are willing to enter into a courtship with you. If a person is divorced and has no annulment, they are presumed married and they should not be courting anyone.

However, often they are not courting; they are just dating. They have no intention of getting married again. Take for instance, the woman who dated a divorced man for several years. Both were Catholic. I asked her if he had sought an annulment, and she said no. I urged her to ask him to do so, but she was afraid. When I saw her a few years later, I asked if he had gotten the annulment. The answer was still no. I told her, "He'll never marry you." That was an unwelcome remark, but the pattern was clear. Here was a man who supposedly loved this woman but was not willing to try to be free to marry her. She was foolish to date him. And, of course, he never did marry her.

Remember too, that not everyone who applies for an annulment gets one. There is no guarantee. It's unwise to get involved with someone who merely has applied for annulment. Wait until they have it in hand before you begin seeing them.

Another issue is involved with regard to divorced persons. Some divorced persons are very good people who have been wronged by their former spouses. However, others are primarily responsible for the divorce, and admitting that is the furthest thing from their mind. You need to be extra careful about getting to know someone who has been divorced and evaluating their character.

While there is a good deal of subjectivism in the latter process, the annulment question is more objective. A person either has one or doesn't. (If they are just applying for one, then they don't have it.) If they don't have an annulment, you want to avoid getting romantically entangled until they do have one. *No annulment equals no dating* is a great rule to stick with. Those who are graciously firm about this save themselves a lot of trouble and wasted time.

Hot and Cold Relationships

Hot and cold relationships, that is, relationships that are wonderful one day and rotten the next are bad news. The problem is that some people are addicted to love, and they can't bring themselves to beak up even with a terrible cad. "Can't live with them; can't live without them." If that's the feeling you have, you must find a way to live without him or her.

One young woman was dating a man who had all the earmarks of a bad match. From what she told me, she could hope for nothing but misery if she married him. He made her cry all the time, he was manipulative, they would have huge arguments. She would break up with him every so often, but within a month they would be back together. I asked her if she had any fun in her life.

"No, just Marvin," she said.

"No wonder you can't break up with him," I said. "You get bored after a few weeks and call him up. You need to get out and do something very enjoyable at least once a week."

"I work all the time," she complained. "I barely have time for any fun."

"Well, you might want to try to find another job," I suggested

She did. . . and she broke up with Marvin shortly after that.

In early adulthood I determined that hot and cold relationships were simply not worth the trouble. "Why should I keep hitting my head against the wall?" I asked myself. "This is masochistic." So, I resolved never to continue such a self-destructive relationship once I became aware of it. No matter how much I "loved" the person, I resolved to forget the whole thing. I wasn't any brighter or cleverer than other people my age. I just had a great friend to help me see things clearly: the Lord (more on that help in a minute).

Marrying Your Best Friend

The person you marry should be your best friend. This is crucial. After thirty or forty years of marriage, physical beauty may fade, but friendship can remain forever. My own mother delighted in the friendship of my father two years before she ever fell in love with him. Friendship is based on sharing the same values and viewpoints. Do you share religious beliefs, moral beliefs, some recreational interests, intellectual interests, interest in the arts, reading, etc.? You can each learn to share each other's interest in some things, but there should be a strong base from the beginning.

Years ago a young couple got married and their friends doubted it would last. Yet every year things got better. A friend asked the secret of their success. The husband attributed it to their anniversary presents. He had been heavily involved in photography before they married, but had given it up since she had no interest in it. For their first anniversary his wife got out the camera and they took some stills together, and then developed them. She whispered to him "This is my anniversary gift to you, dear." She had secretly studied photography so they could do this together.

The next year he took dancing classes, and as they waltzed together on their anniversary, he said, "This is my anniversary present to you, sweetheart." Each year thereafter they would give a similar gift, thereby cementing their friendship more and more. As their friendship grew, their marriage grew stronger.

Of course, spouses don't need to do everything together. It's healthy to have things you do alone. Nevertheless, you should be able to do a number of things together to help build a strong friendship.

Chemistry Has Its Place

You can't manufacture chemistry, but if you think, "Well, Horatio is right in every category, but after two years there is no chemistry," then he is not a good marriage prospect for you. You don't have to experience fireworks every time you see the person, but you should be drawn to them, not repelled by them, although you can sometimes grow into attraction by way of friendship.

On the other hand, how important is it that you are deeply in love with this person, and can hardly stand to be apart? Not very. I was infatuated with a good number of women before I entered the seminary, but often not wisely so. *Eros*, that strong desire for the good, the beautiful and the true in the other, is not nearly as important for marriage as friendship and *agape*, the ability to give oneself unconditionally for the good of the beloved.

Incidentally, if you were a bit more deeply in love with a former sweetheart than you are with the person you are currently with, this does not mean the one you love now is not the right one. You need not have a peak experience every time you're with him/her.

There is no doubt that emotional love has been over-stressed in our culture, especially in the movies, but it's not the end-all and be-all. Nonetheless, it helps if there is a real attraction to the other person.

Appearance Counts . . . Or Does It?

What about flashy women or handsome, cool men? Beware. Flashy women may be manipulators or persons who don't know how to accept good, decent treatment. (Flashy women often do *not* get treated well.) Regarding handsome men, one happily married woman commented to me, "Father, you've got to tell these women they can't all marry a handsome guy. I used to date lots of handsome men, and they treated me horribly. They were all spoiled brats!" When a man is both handsome and "cool" you have double jeopardy. Humility is the key. Is he self-effacing, able to go unnoticed for a while? (This, by the way, is a major ingredient for sanctity.) Or, is he arrogant, and always seeking attention in a group? Quiet men often make great husbands and fathers.

Independence From Parents

Years ago a couple came to me to ask advice about their relationship. She was six years older than he. They were concerned about the age difference. I assured them it wasn't a problem as long as a number of other things were right. The problem was that his parents wouldn't hear of their son marrying an older woman. He was afraid they would disown him if he married her. I told him he had to have the courage to politely say to his parents that he appreciated their concern for his welfare, but he had to make his own decisions. If they rejected him because of that, it was their choice, but that he hoped they would accept him and his decision because he was going to do what he thought was right.

I told the young woman that if he didn't stand up to his parents now, he probably never would, and she should drop him.

Unfortunately, he didn't stand up to them, and the whole thing got messier and messier.

Another man came and asked what I thought of his marrying his fiancée. He said they would be watching TV together and her mother would come in and join them for the evening. He also said that they went out shopping for furniture recently, and the mother came with them and had the major voice in what they bought. I told him he was headed for big trouble. He was marrying two women, not one.

One young woman returned to her home town and told her parents she had met a man who would make a great husband. He was a daily communicant, had a fine personality, and was a genuinely good guy but he was about 12 or 13 years older than she was. Her parents decided the man was too old for her and that she should marry her previous boyfriend, who was not at all religious. So, she went back and started dating him again. God help her.

Another couple had been dating for some time and things were going swimmingly. Then, one weekend when he was taking his mother to Atlantic City, he decided to invite his girlfriend as well. It was a disaster. Both women were annoyed by the end of the weekend. It was the beginning of the end, which occurred some months later.

Parents can often provide great insight into the person you are dating, but they are not always right. In the latter case you must have the courage to tell them, "I appreciate the advice, and I have considered it carefully. But this is ultimately my decision."

Do Opposites Attract?

Do opposites really attract, as they say? Perhaps it's true for magnets, but not for people. Often the thing that most attracted you to someone, the thing that was most different from yourself, is the thing that will drive you batty in marriage. Psychologist Neil Clark Warren writes in *Finding The Love of Your Life*, "Nearly every current psychological study indicates that it's crucial to find a spouse who is a lot like you. If they are different from you, there may be some early attraction, but the most enduring and satisfying marriages are usually ones in which the partners are very much alike."[2]

This makes sense, since friendship is the most important natural ingredient for a good marriage. Since friendship is based on sharing common interests, similarities are very important.

What are some of the key similarities a couple should have for a successful marriage? Certainly religion and morality are key. Personal habits are also important. These include things such as orderliness, dependability, responsibility, and punctuality. I dated a woman once who was, on the average, forty-five minutes late for everything. If that bothers you when you're dating, it will bother you more when you're married. Other key areas include smoking habits, eating habits (health food vs. junk food), energy level, spending patterns, and the ability and willingness to talk. This is not to say that if you have differences in one or two of these areas you should break up. Rather, as Neil Clark Warren says, if you have differences in several of these, or if in a few of these you are *very* different, or if you can't deal with such differences, be cautious. There could indeed be problems.

One of the things that can make up for a number of differences, and any number of other marital problems, is adaptability. This is essential for any relationship, but especially for marriage.

One couple was so busy being involved in studies and jobs that they only discovered on their honeymoon how different they were. They told Neil Clark Warren that if they had not both been raised in large families in which they had to be adaptable, they could not have survived their differences. "Being flexible, instead of unbending, adaptive instead of rigid, can save a couple's marriage from being destroyed by differences. Of course, it takes *two* people willing to compromise and adjust," he explains.

Willingness to Improve

I have worked with many married couples and the one thing that stands out among the successful ones is that they are all trying to do better. They are all trying to grow and to adapt to their spouses.

Sometimes when a woman asks her man to change his behavior, he will say, "Well, that's the way I've always behaved. You have to accept me the way I am." Of course, the woman must look into her own behavior and see if she is asking him to do something unreasonable or if she is just nit-picking. She might discuss the issue with a priest or a close and closed-mouth friend, to make sure her requests are reasonable. Once she becomes convinced that she isn't out of line, it's time to re-evaluate him.

If he has no intention of growing as a person, if he has never apologized for anything, if he has never made any progress in a problem area, he's not a good candidate for marriage.

Of course, it isn't just men who refuse to change. If anyone — man or woman — says, "You'll just have to accept me the way I am," during courtship, and their behavior is significantly unacceptable, that is the time to back off from the whole relationship. Say, "I'm sorry but I can't accept that behavior," and be ready to end things. Better now than later.

Let's Get Intimate

No, this is not about sex. The intimacy I'm referring to here is spiritual or emotional intimacy. Neil Clark Warren says that "Intimacy has the potential for lifting the two of you out of the lonely world of separateness and into the stratosphere of emotional oneness." Psychologists tell us this intimacy is one of the most important ingredients for a good marriage, yet at least one study looked at scores of couples and discovered that only a small percentage experienced real intimacy.

We are all created in the image and likeness of God, the Trinitarian God, the God of three persons. In the Trinity there is a complete intimacy of love between the persons, and in fact the persons themselves are defined only in relation to each other. We discover ourselves and are fulfilled only in relating, to God and to others.[3] But in order to be fulfilling, our relationships must be intimate, not superficial. Who, after all, would really want a superficial relationship with God? In fact, it is precisely such a relationship which makes religion boring.

So it is in marriage. A superficial relationship between husband and wife can be catastrophically boring and unfulfilling. To share intimacy a couple must be able to share their innermost thoughts, desires, feelings, dreams, fears and joys. As Neil Clark Warren says in *Finding The Love of Your Life*:

> It is when this "core" information is revealed that partners become acquainted with each other's inner workings. In this process of discovery, they gain vital information about whether the two of them belong together permanently.

Many of us are moving so fast in life that we may not even have an inner self, an inner person, to share with another. Sometimes our fast-paced society allows us to live life in a superficial way without ever developing any deep, inner thoughts and desires. We never ask: What is most important to me and why? What is my greatest fear? What are my goals in life? What people are most important to me? What are my strengths and weaknesses? Do I want to grow as a person, and how am I pursuing that? How do I feel about friendship, about maturity, about parents, about classmates, about siblings?

These are examples of intimate things we should be able to share with a person once we get to know them. This is not to say we have to make a list of these things and define each one. We may never have articulated them. But when we have time to think about them and we know what we think, we can articulate them when it is appropriate.

(Incidentally, when women have an intimate conversation with their husband before marital relations, they are generally far more responsive. Intimate verbal intercourse fosters intimate sexual intercourse.)

The question here is, does your sweetheart have any depth and can they share it with you? Often men have more trouble with intimacy than women. Sometimes a woman will say, "He never shares anything about his inner self, and he is uncomfortable when I want to share the things that are really important to me." What they sometimes discover is that the man has no inner self because he hasn't developed one. This can be a major problem, something to beware of, as Neil Clark Warren warns.

On the other hand, it could be that a person does have an inner self, but is unwilling, or uninterested in sharing it. This too can be a red flag for a courtship. Intimacy is one thing that can bond a couple together and enable them to become one mind, one flesh. "Intimacy: Don't leave home without it."

Counting the Cost of Money

Income is important only when it is coupled with the right motives. If it's a matter of "It's just as easy to fall in love with a rich man as a poor one," or "I need to find someone who can support me in the lifestyle to which I am accustomed," there's trouble. If a woman wants to marry a man with the earning potential to make it possible for her to be home with their children, that's a noble aspiration. The end result may be the same, but the motive can make a world of difference.

The bottom line is that a man should have a good job in order to get married. If he plans to marry a woman who will support him, she's asking for trouble. A man should be a *man*, fully prepared to support his wife and children. If he's not, he's not ready to get married. How often have we heard of the man who got his wife to put him through medical school or law school, and then ran off with someone else? Such relationships can work in some cases, but the whole idea should be a warning to a woman.

Check Him/Her Out

It's important to see a person in many different situations. Go on a ski weekend together (in a group, with separate rooms!); paint a room together; go camping with friends or chaperones; do volunteer work together; visit a sick friend in the hospital. If all you ever do is go out to dinner or dancing, you won't get to know him/her well.

Place some real importance on how others view this person. What do his/her friends have to say about him/her? What do your parents think? If they have a good record for recognizing character, consider their opinion carefully. However, remember, it's *your* decision, not theirs.

Make a List

After you have gotten to know someone well, and have been seeing each other for a year or so, you might want to make a list of good and bad points. Deciding on a spouse is not the time to be all syrupy. You must be warmly loving, but coldly rational when making this choice. Making a list is a good way to overcome blindness which is, to be sure, a perennial problem even for the most seasoned veterans of courtship.

"What if I could do better?" some think. You could always do better and so could your sweetheart. It's not a matter of finding the best possible spouse, or a perfect one, but a good one who is right for you. Consider the man who divorced his sweet, kind wife to marry a more sophisticated woman. When the second wife divorced him, he admitted, "I divorced my best friend to marry my worst enemy."

Reasonable Expectations

Some people try to be "realistic" about the right spouse, and make concessions on essentials, but are idealistic about the kind of marriage they hope to have. They have it backwards. If you keep your standards high and your expectations moderately low, you won't be disappointed.

One 35-year-old engaged woman asked me, "Father, I'm kind of happy with my life now. I'm not sure I want to get married right away. Do you think I'll be happier when I get married?"

"No," I told her. "Marriage can be hard in the first several years, especially when your children are young."

"Then why should I get married," she asked.

"Because you are building something beautiful for the future. If you work at marriage and family it will be very beautiful in time."

My advice came from the experience of several couples I had dealt with, and the analysis of psychologists who propose that the happiest people are the single women, then married men, married women, and single men. This is at the natural level of life, of course. With a strong spirituality, you can be very happy regardless of your state in life.

Pray Hard But Use Your Head

Because love is terribly blind, even for the wisest of persons, and because you can never be *absolutely* sure that you've found Mr. or Miss Right, prayer must play a huge role in the discernment process. Pray, pray, pray! Pray the daily Rosary, go to Mass daily if possible, get to confession at least once a month. And, of course, live in the state of grace, i.e., no sexual activity. If you live in God's grace, you will have the Holy Spirit and his gift of Counsel. Choosing a spouse is no time to be without the counsel of the Holy Spirit.

When I was in college I dated a smart, attractive girl. She was Catholic, too. Well . . . kind of. She went to Mass every week but she skipped Sunday Mass, and would go during the week. She was also into other types of rebellion. But love is blind. I thought she was "the one." However, when I prayed, I asked God to make things work out if it were his will, and that if it were not, to let me know. It wasn't his will, and he let me know. She broke up with me.

In an emotional fog, I kept thinking that somehow I'd get her back. "I've never loved anyone the way I loved her!" I thought. In the afternoons, with my head in control, I told my heart, "Look, stupid, you're lucky. This woman was trouble and she was not Catholic, in any true sense." But the next morning I would wake up with my heart in control again: "But I love her. What a woman!" By the afternoon my common sense would come alive again and present the reasons why I should forget her. After several weeks of this, inspired by lots of prayer, my emotions gave up. My heart conceded, "Okay, okay, I give up. You're right. She would be trouble."

This experience taught me two things: First, prayer is essential to even have hope of a good choice. And not just any prayer, but prayer specifically asking God to bring about his will. Second, to live reasonably and happily, you must use your head to convince your heart which way to go. If you let your heart lead you'll always be miserable. You must relentlessly hammer away with reason to convince the heart to accept what is right. (This incidentally, is analogous to the way you develop the virtue of chastity.)

Ready. Set. Action!

What should a person do who has prayed, has really taken the time to get to know the other person, and everything is in place?

A man should act decisively. Don't be an indecisive wimp, hoping for an apparition. Trust in God's help and pop the question.

What about the woman in the same situation? What should she do if everything is right, they've been seeing each other for a couple of years, she has decided he is the one, and he doesn't commit, for no apparent reason. Begin by dropping a hint: "I'm beginning to wonder where things are going with us." If nothing comes of that, move on to the next stage, by saying "I think it might be good for us to date other people." If he says, "Why, don't you still love me?" Simply say, "I do, but it seems we have a timing problem. I am ready for commitment and you aren't." This avoids putting pressure on him, while letting him know you are ready for marriage. Incidentally, if he says, "Okay, let's date other people," you need to follow through and do it. Otherwise you may end up like a woman I once knew in her mid-forties who had dated a man for thirteen years before he broke up with her. What a waste of her life. Some men just can't commit. The smart woman accepts that, and when she's waited a reasonable amount of time and he doesn't propose marriage, she moves on.

Women also need to be wary of the man who proposes after only two or three months. One of the most common causes for choosing the wrong spouse is for one or both to be overly eager to get married. I don't care how old you both are or how "together" you think you are, any man who proposes after such a short time may not have the patience to build a good, strong relationship. Tell him to slow down, and you don't want to *think* about marriage until you've courted at least nine months — yes, even if you're 39 years old! In fact, studies show that two years is an ideal amount of time to court before marriage.

Summing It Up

A number of "essentials" should never be compromised when looking for a spouse: solid faith, friendship, no addictions or major hangups, a real interest in raising good children, the ability to communicate, the ability to stand up to controlling parents, some interpersonal chemistry, and a willingness to commit to self-giving love.

Women: avoid the perpetual adolescent, the control freak, the liar. A few years ago Steve Arterburn and Dr. Meg Rink wrote a book entitled, *Avoiding Mr. Wrong.* In it, they tell women to take their time, stop having sex, and study the man carefully. They also list ten types of Mr. Wrong to avoid, including the Mama's boy, the eternal kid, the detached man, the addict, and the ungodly man.

Men: steer clear of the deceiving woman and the manipulator.

Both: Keep your standards reasonably high. It is better to be single and wish you were married than to be married and wish you were single.

This must be a person who will help you to get to heaven. You need to see him/her in a number of different situations, not just dinner and a movie. You should consider the opinions of other people, but sift them with prudence. Above all, stay close to the Lord through prayer, Mass, confession, and living a moral life. Ultimately, only by God's grace can you make the right choice.

Endnotes

1. Vatican II, *Gaudium et spes*, n. 50; and the *Catechism of the Catholic Church*, n. 2373.

2. Neil Clark Warren, *Finding The Love of Your Life*, New York: Simon and Schuster, 1992.

3. In *Gaudium et spes* we read: "The Lord Jesus, when He prayed to the Father, 'that all may be one . . . as we are one' (John 17:21–22) opened up vistas closed to human reason, for He implied a certain likeness between the union of the divine

Persons, and the unity of God's sons in truth and charity. This likeness reveals that man, who is the only creature on earth which God willed for itself, cannot fully find himself except through a sincere gift of himself" (from Walter M. Abbott, S.J., General Editor, The America Press, 1966, n. 24).

Chapter Two

Understanding Love[1]

When I was in my final year of theological studies in the seminary, I took a class called "Inter-seminary Seminar." Theology students from various other nearby seminaries took part, and we would discuss the different theological outlooks of our Faith. I'll never forget the day when we happened on the subject of love and one seminarian claimed that there was no way God can command us to love[2] since love is a feeling and you can't will a feeling. It just has to come. Notwithstanding his arrogance in denying the validity of Scripture, he made the crucial error of misunderstanding the meaning of love in the two great commandments Jesus put forth. The love Jesus speaks of is a willed love, not the love which is felt. As luck would have it, I had been reading C. S. Lewis' book *The Four Loves* and explained to him the different loves, and how, when properly understood, Jesus could indeed command love.

That was when I first discovered the confusion that exists among English-speaking people regarding the subject of love. I found the same confusion one day when I was discussing with a parishioner her relationship with her husband. She said she really didn't love him much anymore. I asked her if she was concerned for his good, and she replied she was. "Then," I said, "you love him. *That* is the love you pledged on your wedding day, not some romantic feeling. When you tell him you love him, that should be the primary meaning of the love you profess."

"I haven't told him I love him in a long time," she admitted.

"Well, don't you think you should? After all you promised to love him for as long as you both shall live."

"I don't know if I can bring myself to say it now," she answered.

Clearly he had hurt her over the years, and she believed she had to feel love before she could say it. Oddly enough, couples often come to feel love again only when they say it and work at it again. In any event, here was another example of confusion over the meaning of love. I have encountered many other instances of this confusion over the years, some of which have been nearly catastrophic.

In order to understand Christian courtship, it's important to try to eliminate the confusion in the English language regarding the different meanings of love. There are, alas, several meanings of the word love, for which the Greeks had four different words. The first, *agape* ("ah-gáh-pay"), is often translated as "divine love" because it is typified by the self-sacrificial love of God for mankind. The second, *philia*, is friendship, sometimes called brotherly love. The third, *storge* ("stór-gay"), is affection, often called familial love. The fourth, *eros*, is emotional love. As I mentioned earlier, C. S. Lewis wrote a classic explanation of these four dynamics of love. I will use some of his ideas as a starting point herein.

'Agape' (Divine Love)

The love which a man and woman pledge for each other on their wedding day is divine love, or as the Greek called it, *agape*. This is the most important of the four loves since it is the condition for salvation: "You shall love the Lord your God with all your heart, with all your soul, with all your strength, and with all your mind. . . ." (Luke 10:27). The Greek word used here is *agapao*, a derivative of *agape*. Since it is a command, it must be a voluntary act, not a feeling. We might define it as *a giving of self for the good of the beloved without conditions*. Another way to put it would be *an active concern for the good of the beloved which is unconditional*.

If you love in this way, you give of your time, your money, your effort, whatever you have, for the one you love. But you don't give indiscriminately. You give only insofar as it is for the *good* of the one you love. Giving so as to please the other may be divine love, but not always, since what pleases a person is not necessarily what is good for him or her.

The father who says no to his son when he asks for a Mercedes on his sixteenth birthday is showing him love. The woman who says no to her boyfriend when he asks for immoral activity is showing him love. The parent who refuses to provide housing to his drug-dealing son is giving him "tough love." God himself gives us tough love when we turn from his way and our life falls apart.

There are no "ifs" in this sort of love. "If you behave," or "if you continue to please me," or "if you don't get fat," have no place here. Parents must love their children in this consistent way, always ready to work for their good, whether the children please them or not.

God himself doesn't like us much when we sin, but he will always take us back, because he is a God of love. His active concern for our good involves no conditions, and he expects us to love in the same way.

Agape is usually expressed in quiet, enduring ways, without much fanfare. Fifty years of doing a family's laundry; forty years of ministering to the sick and dying; decades of little sacrifices for spouse and children; a life-long commitment to prayer, and teaching young children. As such, this is the least exciting, and even potentially boring of the loves. But it is the most powerful and most rewarding in the long run.

It's like watering a small tree. You carry water to it and care for it day after day, week after week, year after year, and the growth is hardly noticeable. Then one day, after many years, the tree blossoms, and finally bears fruit. It is only then, after all that seemingly endless effort, that you come to realize it was all worth it. In fact this love is the only thing that can fulfill us as persons. Pope John Paul II wrote in *Redemptor hominis*:

> Man cannot live without love. He remains a being that is incomprehensible for himself, his life is senseless, if love is not revealed to him, if he does not encounter love, if he does not experience it and make it his own, if he does not participate intimately in it.

We see this agape love in the wife or husband who has been deeply disappointed by his/her spouse, and yet puts that aside to try to make peace and heal the relationship. We see it in those who have been married 25 years or more. They've been through the years together, the hurts so typical of any human relationship, the trials, and the hardships. And now, because their love was truly unconditional, and they continued to love when it ceased being fun, they have something special. There's a certain peace, a glow in their marriage. This is the way of *agape*.

I'll never forget the woman whose husband I visited because he was dying of cancer. He had left her some years before, and gone to live with a younger woman. When he got sick and his young consort wanted nothing more to do with him, his wife took him in. She cared for him until he died. She understood the power of agapaic love.

Although *agape* is an outward movement, a giving of self, those who love in this way ordinarily receive as well.[3] So, even though *agape* most often involves receiving as well as giving, the Christian will always emphasize giving more than receiving.

The most profound expression of this divine love is to give "when it hurts." Christ put it very directly: "A man can have no greater love than to lay down his life for his friends" (John 15:13). He preached this love, and he lived, and died by it. By his grace, we too can live, and die by it.

Conjugal or Choice Love (a type of 'agape')

The verb form of *agapao*, is occasionally used in the New Testament to speak of a choice. Christ said: "No man can serve two masters. He will either hate one and love the other or be attentive to one and despise the other" (Matthew 6:24). That is to say, he will *choose* either one or the other. Thus there is a love which might be called "choice love" or choice *agape*. It is this love we are to have for God, for he would have us choose him above all other gods we might fashion. Our love for God should have four marks: first, *permanence*, in that it should be an ever-lasting commitment; second, *exclusiveness*, in that we should love no other person to the extent that we love God, i.e., with all our heart, soul, and mind; third, *public*, in that we should give witness to this love to others; and fourth, *fruitful*, in that it should bear fruit in our sharing God's life in us, the life of grace.

Although this choice love is unique, another love reflects it: the conjugal love of marriage. Conjugal love is meant to have the same four marks: *permanence*, in that it should be a lifelong commitment; *exclusiveness*, in that each has but one spouse; *public*, in that couples marry in public and make known their commitment, living it out in public; and *fruitful*, in that it is ordered to the begetting of new life.[4] In these ways the conjugal love in marriage symbolizes to the world the (conjugal) love between a person and God.[5]

While conjugal or choice *agape* can be expressed in any of the ways *agape* is expressed, there is one way which is unique to it: bodily communion. With the Lord this involves receiving the Eucharist. With spouses it involves sexual intercourse.

The Eucharist is, of course, a crown for committing to love God above all things, and a source of grace to keep that commitment. Christopher West proposes a similar analogy in *Good News about Sex and Marriage*:

> Where do we become one flesh with Christ? Most specifically in the Eucharist. The Eucharist is the sacramental consummation of the marriage between Christ and the Church. And when we receive the body of your heavenly bridegroom into our own, just like a bride we conceive new life in us — God's very own life.

Sexual intimacy is a sacred, physical sign of the conjugal *agape* of marriage. As such, it shares the same four marks:

1. Permanence. The sex act itself cries out for a tomorrow. No matter what prior agreement has been made, if a true commitment does not exist between the partners, i.e., marriage, there will likely be at least a wistful feeling afterwards.

2. Exclusiveness. No one who is truly in love would be comfortable sharing his or her sex partner.
3. Public. Although the act of intercourse does not ordinarily take place in public (thank goodness), husband and wife don't usually hide the fact that they sleep together.
4. Fruitful. The act is ordered toward accepting nature's offer of new life. Children are the fruit of married love and give witness to that love for all eternity.

Why is there so much pleasure in sex? What's the purpose of this pleasure? The most obvious reason for pleasure in sex is to encourage the propagation of the human race. However, this cannot be the only reason, since the sex act and its pleasure are licit and good during those times when procreation is impossible — for example, after menopause, during infertile times, or in the case of sterility.

I would submit, therefore, that the pleasure of sex is also intended as an encouragement to make the commitment of conjugal love and to keep it. Vatican II taught:

> This [conjugal] love is uniquely expressed and perfected through the act proper to marriage. Hence, the actions within marriage by which the couple are united intimately and chastely are noble and worthy. Expressed in a manner which is truly human, these actions signify and foster the mutual self-donation by which spouses enrich each other with a joyful and a ready mind.[6]

Marital intimacy, then, symbolizes and "fosters" the continued conjugal love commitment of man and wife.

Sexual communion is both a crown and a source. It is a crown for making the commitment of conjugal love, and a source of encouragement to keep that commitment.

'Philia' (Friendship)

As C. S. Lewis rightly suggests, friendship (*philia*) is essentially a relationship based on sharing a common interest. If two people share the same faith, the same politics, the same taste in music, in entertainment, in sports, in intellectual pursuits, they are likely to enjoy spending time together. Lewis rightly points out that while *eros* is face to face, friendship is "side by side." It is best when shared with more than one because, again as Lewis explains, there is an aspect of Doug that is brought out only by John or Don. And Doug brings out something in Don that John does not. Philia can be cultivated, or it may just happen. Additionally, it can be between any ages, any sexes.

Moderation is the key to a lasting friendship. Like a flower, it will be crushed if it is clung to too tightly; it will wither if it is neglected for too long. We should keep up with friends, but never smother them.

Some friendships fade because people change, and go different ways. If this happens, the friendship need not be mourned but be remembered with warmth and gratitude. But when a friendship grows old and mellow like a fine wine, it should be treasured.

Ordinarily, friends contribute more or less equally to the relationship. However, at times one or the other may be unable to give equally. This is when *agape*, that self-giving love which is the support of all the loves, must take over. A friend is there for his or her friend in time of need. During such a time that person may receive nothing at all from the friendship, except perhaps the knowledge that the relationship was more than a business deal. Thus it becomes an image of our friendship with God.

St. Augustine held friendship to be the highest of the three human loves (*agape* being divine). Indeed, which of the human loves could be more important to a marriage? To share the same faith, the same education, the same values, the same recreational interests, the same tastes — these are things on which good marriages are built and without which they may suffer. For him to take dancing lessons because she loves to dance, for her to study football because he loves the game are ways to build a friendship for the sake of the committed conjugal love of marriage.

This is not to say married people shouldn't have things they do separately, without their spouse, but there should be many things they do together, to reinforce their friendship bond.

Friendship is expressed by sharing feelings with one another, the joys of victory, and if the friendship is deep, the sorrows of defeat. It involves risk and perhaps even hurt, but it's worth the risk and hurt to find true friendship.

For a married couple, the friendship should be deep. In other words, each should be able to share their deepest inner thoughts and desires, their feelings, their hopes and fears. To share these things takes a great deal of trust, so you don't generally go into them on the third date. But as familiarity and trust begin to grow, the couple should want to share these deep feelings with each other, and discover what they have in common.

To speak of intimate things, each must be interested in the words of the other. When you pour out your heart to someone and they respond, "Where shall we go for dinner tomorrow?" you know there's a problem. Each person must respect and want to support the other.

If there's fear of rejection, the words of intimacy won't flow. And, as Neil Clark Warren points out, when these things are shared, there's careful listening and real openness. Those who meditate a great deal in prayer, who are comfortable with silence and need not have the radio or television going at all times, who read — especially spiritual books — are generally much more prepared for intimacy than those who do not do these things. This is another reason why religion is so important in a potential spouse. Religion, that is really practicing religion, helps to prepare people for intimacy, which gives love its depth.

The sharing of intimacy occurs most easily when the two are alone together in an appropriate setting. Going out to dinner and sitting in a secluded part of a quiet restaurant can be a great place for this, as is going on a long walk on the beach. Certainly times of crisis or loss often lend themselves to intimate conversation. Couples who have shared their failures and struggles will generally have a far more intimate relationship than those who have not. A man and woman should have an intimate friendship before they ever speak of marriage.

One of the most important things a married couple shares is raising children. Children are a wonderful common interest of parents, and can contribute greatly to their friendship. Children should never be seen as interfering with the love of parents, but as fostering it. This is why couples should not delay having children to give themselves "time to get to know each other," which often means "time to enjoy each other without interference." Children will draw the parents more deeply into that self-giving *agape*, which is the source of all happiness, and more deeply in friendship, the highest of the human loves. Love which tries to exclude others even for a short time without an important reason fosters selfishness.

Some of the best marriages start with friendship, not courtship. In fact, a number of young people, as evidenced by Joshua Harris' book, *Boy Meets Girl*, choose to develop a friendship with someone they like. Then, if the friendship flourishes, the young man proposes a courtship. This is a great way to remove the tremendous pressure modern dating puts on couples. Contemporary dating is often more a preparation for divorce than it is for marriage![7]

What a precious thing is friendship! "A faithful friend is a sturdy shelter: he that has found one has found a treasure . . . A faithful friend is an elixir of life; and those who fear the Lord will find [one]" (Sirach 6:14).

'Storge' (Affection)

Affection is sometimes called familial love because it commonly occurs among family members, but it is most important in courtship as well. It is a tenderness, a gentle caring for someone.

Affection is expressed in many ways: a hug; a tender kiss on the lips, the cheek, or forehead; a tender smile; a gentle touch on the arm, the hand, the hair. It seems that good, selfless, chaste affection has been a casualty in our over-sexed world. Many have lost the art of affection.

We all have a need for affection — a tender look, a touch. Such affection is found between parent and child, a wife and husband, a girl and her best friend. At the right place and time, an affectionate touch is a beautiful way to communicate love, sometimes the *only* way.

Years ago Ann Landers took a survey of her married women readers, asking whether they would prefer to be "cuddled" or to have intercourse. Over 70 percent preferred to be cuddled. I don't think this is because they didn't like intercourse, but because they hadn't been cuddled in a long time.

Often wives tell me that all their husbands want to do is have sex. When I ask if they had sex before marriage, the answer is inevitably yes. Therein lies the problem. Such couples never developed the habit of sharing affection together, as an end in itself. When a man has sex with his woman before marriage, he often sees kissing and touching as merely an introduction to sexual intercourse. These wives need to help their husbands realize the importance of affection in a good marriage. Husbands and wives need to be able to touch, hug, kiss and be kissed without this being a prelude to sexual activity. Affection is an important language of love, one that should be learned well during courtship.

So often, when chastity is discussed in a religious context, the sharing of affection is barely covered. Because of that, young people are rightly confused about what is acceptable and what isn't. So often we speak endlessly about what you shouldn't do, without making a positive proposal about what you should do.

One young man about 30 years old called me after one of our "Christian Dating in An Oversexed World" seminars, and asked, "Well, Father, what *should* I do to tell my sweetheart goodnight?"

I told him, "Well, you might put your hand to her face and move forward ever-so-slowly, and gently kiss her. Once. Twice. Then give her a big, slow hug, pressing your cheek against hers and feeling the warmth as a way of proclaiming your real warm feelings for her. Then, perhaps say something nice, such as, 'You are so precious to me,' and put your hand to her face again. Then say goodnight and kiss her once more, slowly, tenderly, as if you fear she might break if you aren't careful."

"Not bad, Father."

"It's been a while, but I have a good memory."

Is there more to romantic affection than just a goodnight kiss? Absolutely. If a couple has been going out for a while, he might give her a brief, but tender kiss on the cheek, and a hug when he comes to pick her up. He might kiss her hand from time to time. He might touch her face on occasion or her hand when they walk. He might put his arm around her shoulder at times, or touch her hair. Slow, gentle hugs are powerfully symbolic chaste acts of unity.

She should be able to show affection to him as well, especially if he has given her reason to be confident in his love for her. She might put her head on his shoulder while watching a movie. Or, she might touch him gently on the hand or kiss him gently on the cheek. Another possibility would be to take his hand and put it around her waist, or just put her arm in his, and lean lightly against him, as they walk along.

One good Catholic man said he shared affection with his girl-friend by having her sit on the couch while he would lie with his head on her lap. They would talk for hours as he played with her hand and, he said, they shared real spiritual intimacy, so important to a good marriage. I told him, "Fine, as long as you don't change positions!"

This should pretty much be the extent of physical expressions of love in courtship. Imagine how spiritually and psychologically healthy courtship would be if this were the accepted norm for sharing affection.

Remember, in sharing affection moving slowly is usually indicative of giving, of honoring and serving the beloved. Moving more rapidly or touching more intensely is usually indicative of seeking, of pleasing and serving the self.

Freedom in Moderation

Now, for some, this may be a big step back. But, it's a healthy one. Many people who have taken it are glad they did. The problem is that in our Western world we have a hedonistic attitude toward pleasure that says, if it's pleasant I must gorge myself on it. Nowadays, when something is pleasurable, we tend to want to have our fill of it, to be completely sated with it. If we like to ski, we become "avid skiers." If we like tennis, we become "tennis addicts." If we enjoy kissing, it's a given we will sleep together.

That, of course, is not the Christian way. The Christian approach to pleasure is to delight in it for the moment, and then forget about it, to enjoy something without becoming attached to it. In other words, to not desire any thing or any person outside God to the point that you can't be happy without it. This is why St. Francis of Assisi would only see St. Clare once a year; he enjoyed her friendship so much he didn't want to depend on it for his happiness.

What a blessing it is to be able to enjoy the little tastes of joy in life, seeing in them a small whisper of the joy of heaven, without having to be a slave to them, even in a small way. In other words, the real Christian can be satisfied with little pleasures, whether in food, or drink, or a goodnight kiss, or even the joy of friendship, without insisting on having more.

The place of complete satiation,[8] of deep fulfillment is not this world, but the next. If we can savor the little delights and pleasures we encounter along the way and be content with them, we can be at peace as we journey towards complete and final fulfillment in the divine marriage of God's Kingdom.

Wherever you set your threshold for satisfaction — at the small delights that come from a warm, chaste hug or kiss, or the intense pleasure that comes from having premarital sex several times a week — you will be equally unfulfilled. Why? Because our desires are infinite, and if we try to fulfill them with finite things we will never arrive at fulfillment. The more we give our appetites, whether it be for exotic foods, or liquor, or sex, the more they want. If we set our pleasure threshold at a licit level, we'll be just as psychologically fulfilled as if we set it at a hedonistic level. However, setting it at a licit level will enable us to be detached from pleasure, and make us free to give ourselves in unselfish love (*agape*), without being enslaved to our passions and using others to satisfy them.

Women: Ask for What You Want!

When I mentioned romantic affection to a group of young women, one asked, "Father, that's what we want. Are there any men who do this?"

"No, not many, not yet," I answered. "You have to help them get there."

Women, tell men what you like and don't like. If they're smart, they'll respond. One of my pre-seminary days sweethearts said, "I love it when you touch my face." I'm not a rocket scientist, but I knew enough to keep touching her face in those special moments of sharing affection. Ladies, it's not manipulation to ask for what you like; it's teaching a man how to treat you right. It's only manipulation if you try to make him do things he doesn't like to do. What if he won't treat you the way you like with regard to affection, or anything else, for that matter? Tell him goodbye!

It's no wonder so many couples never develop intimacy during their courtship. They're too busy kissing and hugging (among other things), when they should be talking about the deep things of their heart.

Postponing Kissing Until Marriage?

What about people like Joshua Harris, [9] who decided not to kiss until he married, or Elisabeth Elliot[10] and Steve Wood[11] whose first kisses came with their respective engagements? Are their approaches the best way?

I can understand why they might take that course, since so many good things such as affection, have become sexualized and thus exploitive. But I think their approaches are overreactions to our oversexed culture. There is a great need to rehabilitate affection in our world, to restore it to its proper place, to purify it of its sexual connotations. Affection when it is pure and noble is a beautiful thing. When a couple puts off kissing, even the most innocent sort, until marriage or engagement, they may be implicitly conceding that affection is just a milder form of sexual exploitation. It isn't. It's a wonderful expression of love and it fulfills a human need.

What about affection in public? Please, very little, and only in the right places. Holding hands while taking a walk, briefly kissing goodbye or hello, hugging at the airport, or holding hands at dinner are fine, but ongoing caressing or repeated kissing are personal things that belong in private. Practicing good manners has primarily to do with making others feel comfortable. When a man and woman can hardly keep their hands off each other in public, it is really discomforting for everyone else.

Affection, as Karol Wojtyla (Pope John Paul II) wrote in Love and Responsibility, is not aimed at enjoyment, "but the feeling of nearness."[12] Sharing affection, "has the power to deliver love from the various dangers implicit in the egoism of the senses. . . ." Affection is an important "factor of love," but requires an "inner self-control."

Occasionally a person discovers his or her sweetheart has little use for affection; he/she has difficulty embracing or touching. Sometimes this reticence is due to a fear of sexual advances in our sex-soaked culture. Or, it could be that he/she comes from a family where outward expressions of affection were rare. In either case, I would recommend discussing this delicately and diplomatically, and explaining the importance of trying to gradually ease into a habit of sharing chaste affection. This is something that can be learned, but it must be done gradually, without any outside pressure.

A third possible reason for being affection-shy is a psychological block due to a bad experience in the past. In this case, for their own good, and that of their future spouse and children, they should consider getting some counseling to get at the root problem. Often such a problem can cause major difficulties with loving fully or trusting. Getting counseling from a good, skilled Christian counselor can be extremely beneficial.

To be sure, cultural background has a huge impact on the ability to share affection. Generally the Latins, Philippinos, and some Eastern Europeans are quite comfortable with hugging and kissing among family members and friends. This does not mean that those from other backgrounds should be satisfied with minimal affection. Many studies show that sharing affection physically is quite therapeutic for everyone, regardless of nationality.

It is also important to be affectionate with children. As Gary Smalley indicates in his excellent book for parents *The Blessing*, ". . . meaningful touching can protect a child from looking to meet this need in all the wrong places." Jesus himself had the children come to him, " . . . he took them in his arms, laid his hands on them and blessed them" (Mark 10:16). Pope John Paul II goes so far as to say children have a "special right to [affection]."

Smalley also points out that meaningful touch brings physiological benefits, lowers blood pressure and can add two years to the life of a husband.

Many fathers do not hug or kiss their daughters once they become teenagers. Perhaps this is because as their daughters begin to develop into women, they feel it might be exploitive to show them physical affection. Not so. It speaks volumes for a father to give his daughter a good, chaste hug. Psychologists who have dealt with the sad consequences in daughters whose fathers did not hug them, are united in strongly encouraging this.

So, men, when you become fathers, remember the importance of affection for your daughters and for your sons as well. With discretion and sensitivity, affection is a real plus at any age.

Affection: it's a great aid for mental well-being and a great thing in courtship.

'Eros' (Emotional Love)

The fourth of the "four loves" is emotional love, or *eros*. It means to be well pleased by someone or something, to like very much. We sometimes use love in this sense to describe our feelings about a new stereo, a new car or house: "I just love it!" What we really mean is that we *like* it a great deal, but somehow it doesn't suffice to say, "I like it very much!" "Love" in the English language has come to be a superlative of "like."

In courtship, emotional love means infatuation, the emotional attraction for another which seems, but is not, uncontrollable. Pope John Paul II remarked in his talks on the theology of the body, "According to Plato, 'eros' represents the interior force that attracts man towards everything good, true, and beautiful. . . ."[13] And so, in our context, it means that strong desire for the good, the true, and the beautiful in the other. This is the strongest emotional feeling of attraction short of a mystical experience. It is being "in love."

Eros is not merely sexual desire as Freud mistakenly taught, although sexual attraction may play a part. It is primarily personal. One desires to possess the whole person, not just the body. As such it is far more powerful than sexual attraction.

What is the purpose of this love? Most likely it is designed to be a catalyst for marriage, helping couples overcome hesitancy in making the lifelong commitment of marriage.

In fact, it is probably the prime inducement to marry, although as Hollywood lovers have proven time and again, not the prime ingredient for successful marriage. I remember hearing an actress in the sixties commenting on television about her fourth marriage. "This," she cooed, "is real love. The others were not. This marriage will last because our love is authentic." A few years later that marriage was on the rocks as well.

C. S. Lewis makes a point we would do well to remember: if you make a god out of *eros* it will become a demon and destroy you. *Eros* is a wonderful, marvelous thing, but it is only finite; it is not God. It apes God, insofar as it is so far above other earthly joys that it seems to be a god, but it is not. God alone is infinite, everlasting. *Eros* is neither.

When I was in the seminary, I heard the story of a woman who told a priest that she thought she was in love with him. When he calmly told her that such things can happen, she asked him how he could treat it so lightly. He gently explained to her that falling in love is not the end of the world. Emotions go where they will, but if you don't cultivate the feeling of eros, it will fade in time. And it did.

If you know how finite this god-imitating love is, and realize you don't need to surrender to it whenever it pops up, you will avoid lots of misery. Nonetheless, when it is shared with your spouse and it is understood for what it is, it is very sweet.

Emotional love invariably fades in any relationship for two reasons. First, it thrives on mystery, and mystery fades with familiarity. Second, as a human love, it is limited and needs to be nourished and sustained by divine love. If it is not divinized, it will die as all things merely human must die.

How does one keep it alive — even if not at a wedding day high — in marriage? First by growing and enriching oneself in virtue and knowledge, thereby preserving some mystery in the relationship. Second, by practicing divine love (*agape*). In these ways emotional love, good in itself, can be kept alive, and the relationship retains a certain pizzazz.

Emotional love can be expressed by words: "I'm in love with you," or actions. But by what actions? Passionate acts for passionate feelings? To extend this reasoning to other feelings would require angry acts for angry feelings (perhaps throwing a chair or two, or breaking a few windows), and jealous acts for jealous feelings (perhaps a punch in the mouth). Granted, feelings should be expressed, but in a constructive, reasonable way.

Passionate acts and their natural conclusion, sexual intercourse, signify something much deeper than a feeling. They symbolize commitment, exclusiveness, a total self-gift. They symbolize a love so rich that it wishes to bring forth new life with whom to share that love.

The most honest physical expression of emotional love is romantic affection. This way of touching, hugging, and kissing expresses a pure gratitude and delight in the happiness of this other who has brought such happiness to me. This is the Christian way of expressing *eros*, stripped of the selfishness that kills all love, and divinized by divine love. And it is this expression of *eros* that, because divinized, will enable it to last.

In the Eucharist we find the promise of fulfillment of the natural impulse of emotional love: the consummation of the beloved. In receiving the Eucharist we consume our God as he consumes us more and more into his life of grace, as a sign of the all-consuming love which awaits us in his Kingdom. Emotional love, then, is a sign of the overwhelming fire with which our entire being will burn at the mere sight of God who created and sustains in his own image the creatures for whom our hearts burn in this world.

Incidentally, the word *eros* does not appear in the New Testament, but in the Old Testament, the *Song of Songs* is full of it. It is the story of a passionate love between God and his people:

> You have ravished my heart, my sister, my bride;
> you have ravished my heart with one glance of your eyes,
> with one bead of your necklace.
> How beautiful is your love, my sister, my bride,
> how much more delightful is your love than wine,
> and the fragrance of your ointments than all spices!
> Your lips drip honey, my bride,
> sweetmeats and milk are under your tongue;
> And the fragrance of your garments
> is the fragrance of Lebanon.
> You are an enclosed garden, my sister, my bride,
> an enclosed garden, a fountain sealed.
> You are a park that puts forth pomegranates,
> with all choice fruits. (Song 4:9-12, NAB)

As Bishop Fulton J. Sheen used to say, "Every man promises what only God can give. And every woman promises what only God can give." It is only when a person realizes this that he or she can enjoy *eros* without becoming its slave.

And, moreover, we can all develop a passionate love for God here on earth. Although this is a concept foreign to most Christians, St. Augustine expressed it well:

> Late have I loved you, O Beauty so ancient and so new. I rushed headlong after these things of beauty which you made. They kept me far from you, those fair things which, were they not in you, would not exist at all. You have sent forth fragrance, and I have drawn in my breath, and I pant for you. I have tasted you, and I hunger and thirst for you. You have touched me and I have burned for your peace.

Summing It Up

Each of the four types of love has its own place in our lives. All four are good in their right place. Only *agape* is divine and gives life to all the others. The three human loves wither and die in selfishness if they are not animated by divine love. If *agape* becomes, by grace, the pervasive theme of your life, two things will happen. First, you will begin to love as God loves, something you will delight to see. Second, you will be able to unite in love with God and others. No other earthly delight can exceed that of good relationships. Nothing else will bring lasting happiness, in courtship, in marriage, or in heaven.

Endnotes

1. This chapter is an adaptation of an article by the author which was published in *Fidelity* Magazine in April 1984 entitled "A Basis for Positive Sex Education." Much of it was also published in expanded form in the author's monthly column, "Love Lines" in *New Covenant* Magazine between July 2001 and January 2002.

2. The Lord gives us the two great commandments of love in Mark 12:29–31: To love God with all our heart, soul, and mind; and to love our neighbor as ourselves.

3. If loving a person in this way does not bring about a response because of a lack on the part of the beloved, God promises us a reward nonetheless.

4. Pope Paul VI speaks of conjugal love of having certain marks: human, total, faithful, exclusive until death, and fecund (fruitful) in *Humanae vitae* (n. 9). I added public as another mark which, although less theological, seems to fit our practical discussion here.

5. As described in Isaiah 62: 4–6

6. *Gaudium et spes*, n. 49. (Translation from the Latin is mine.)

7. See Connie Marshner, "Contemporary Dating as Serial Monogamy," *Homiletic and Pastoral Review*, October 1998, p. 18.

8. In heaven, as God the Father explained to St. Catherine in her *Dialogue*, "[The soul] always desires Me [God] and loves me, and her desire is not in vain — being hungry she is satisfied, and being satisfied she has hunger, but the tediousness of satiety and the pain of hunger are far from her." (*The Dialogue of St. Catherine of Siena*, Rockford IL: TAN Books, 1974, p. 110.)

9. Joshua Harris, *Boy Meets Girl*, Sisters, Oregon: Multnomah Publishers, 2000. This is a refreshingly Christian book of some poetic beauty about Joshua's late 90's romance.

10. Elisabeth Elliot, *Passion and Purity*, Grand Rapids, MI: Fleming H. Revell, 1984. For her rationale, see p. 130. Elliot's book is a delightfully poetic, unflinchingly Christian story of her own romantic courtship. Alas, on the issue of kissing, she seems a bit too conservative.

11. Steve Wood, *The ABCs of Choosing A Good Husband*, Port Charlotte, FL: Family Life Center Publications, 2001. Even though Steve and his eventual wife kissed only after they got engaged, Steve now recommends waiting until marriage. (He has done some fine work in promoting Catholic Family Life. See his web site, www.familylifecenter.net.)

12. Karol Wojtyla (Pope John Paul II), *Love and Responsibility*, (New York: Farrar, Straus and Giroux, 1981; now in print by Ignatius Press, San Francisco) p. 203. The translator uses the word "tenderness" but in fact, the clear meaning from the text (and the Polish) is "affection."

13. Pope John Paul II, *Blessed are the Pure of Heart*. (This is contrary to the contemporary, Freudian connotation given to *eros*, that of mere sexual attraction.)

Chapter Three

A Major Challenge: A Chaste Courtship

Perhaps the greatest challenge facing single Christians today is trying to live a chaste, Christian life and courtship. What does Jesus Christ expect of us in courtship in the twenty-first century? The most evident norms are found in Sacred Scripture. Others require reasoning and the guidance of the Church.

Scripture

First, the Scriptural teaching of Jesus on pre-marital sex: "from within, out of the heart of man, come evil thoughts, *fornication*, theft, murder, adultery, coveting, wickedness, deceit, licentiousness, envy. . . . All these evil things come from within, and they defile a man" (Mark: 7:21) (author emphasis).

Fornication is not a word most of us use every day. It is defined as *voluntary sexual intercourse between an unmarried person and another unmarried person of the opposite sex*. In other words, pre-marital sex. So, it's clear Jesus was opposed to pre-marital sex.

In fact, so was St. Paul:

Do you not know that the unjust will not inherit the kingdom of God? Do not be deceived; neither *fornicators* nor
idolaters nor adulterers nor boy prostitutes nor sodomites nor
thieves nor the greedy nor drunkards nor slanderers nor rob-
bers will inherit the kingdom of God. (1 Corinthians 6:9-
10, NAB) (author emphasis)

The word fornication appears three times in the Old Testament,
14 times in the New. In every case it is proclaimed immoral. Exclu-
sion from the kingdom is not the penalty for venial sin. So, clearly,
fornication is a matter of mortal sin. Fornication will keep you out
of the kingdom.

This is not to say that everyone who has fornicated is lost. The
Lord forgives those who repent of this sin and reform. This is clear
from the way he treated the woman caught in adultery in John
8:3–11, and the way he treated Mary Magdalene who, according to
St. Gregory, many believe to be a reformed sinner. Nonetheless,
anyone who loves the Lord, and seeks his/her own good, will make
every attempt to avoid such sins.

Sexual sins are not the worst of serious sins, but they are the
most popular. It is best to avoid all sin, but better to commit the sin
of sexual immorality out of weakness than to commit the sin of
denying the teaching of Scripture that fornication is a sin. In other
words, those who rationalize their fornication and pretend to be
good Christians are far worse than those who embrace the truth,
but fail to live it at times. Since the Scriptures and the teachings of
the Church are so clear on this, claiming innocence through igno-
rance of the issue is almost impossible.

The Church

The Church confirms the teaching of Sacred Scripture in the *Declaration on Sexual Ethics*: "The use of the sexual function has its true meaning and moral rightness only in true marriage." Additionally, it confirms the seriousness of sexual sins: "The moral order of sexuality involves such high values of human life that every direct violation of this order is objectively serious." Thus all sexual activity outside of marriage — including pre-marital sex, adultery, masturbation, and homosexual acts — is seriously sinful.

Why is sex outside of marriage wrong? Briefly, it's immoral because sex is a symbol of committed marital love and sex may produce children who should be conceived and raised in the stable love community of marriage.

How Far Is Too Far?

Premarital sex is clearly wrong. What about other things such as foreplay? Are these things sinful? Yes, any directly intended sexual arousal outside marriage is wrong. St. Thomas Aquinas wrote in the *Summa Theologica*:

> . . . since fornication is a mortal sin, and much more so the other kinds of lust, it follows that in such like sins not only consent to the act but also consent to the pleasure is a mortal sin. Consequently when . . . kisses and caresses are done for this delight, it follows that they are mortal sins. . . . Therefore in so far as they are lustful, they are mortal sins.

St. Thomas defines lust as "seeking sexual pleasure not in accord with right reason." Lust, of course, would include intending or imagining sexual sins, as Jesus pointed out in Matthew 5:28: ". . . I say to you that every one who looks at a woman lustfully has already committed adultery with her in his heart."

Thus, passionate kissing or any other act which by nature or intent stimulates the desire for sex or causes sexual arousal would be categorized as sexual activity. Such an act is ordinarily done to provide a certain incomplete pleasure which can be completed only by sexual intercourse or orgasm. As St. Thomas said, all of these things are seriously sinful.

But why is sexual arousal wrong outside of marriage? Because sexual arousal prepares a person for sexual intercourse. It is unreasonable to prepare for sexual intercourse if you are not planning to have sexual intercourse. Sin is, in its essence, acting contrary to right reason, the reason of God. When a couple get worked up sexually, and then they either back off with a will of steel or come to a climax with some sort of genital activity, they trivialize sex. In other words, they use sex for play. The Church has never trivialized sex, but upholds it as precious and sacred. Thus it can't trivialize the acts to prepare for it either.

So how far does a true Christian go on a date? The principle, simply put, is that sharing affection is generally fine and good, even desirable, but acts which by their nature or intent cause sexual arousal in either person are immoral.

Some have argued that the question of how far you may go on a date is like asking how close you may come to the edge of a cliff without falling off. Not so. Drawing near to the edge of a cliff has no intrinsic value. Sharing affection on a date does. This is a healthy thing, one which helps bonding. As such, it should be pursued reasonably.

Pope John Paul II, in his pre-papal, and widely-acclaimed *Love and Responsibility*, notes that affection (or in his words, "tenderness") is an important factor in love, but that "there can be no genuine tenderness without a perfected habit of continence," or self-control, "which has its origin in a will always ready to show loving kindness, and so overcome the temptation merely to enjoy. . . ." In other words, there is a line between the good and noble exchange of affection and the seeking of sexual pleasure. To stay on the moral side of that line requires self-control.

A Note About Pornography

Is viewing pornography for recreation seriously sinful? Yes, because it corrupts the mind. The *Catechism of the Catholic Church* teaches:

> Pornography consists in removing real or simulated sexual acts from the intimacy of the partners, in order to display them deliberately to third parties. It offends against chastity because it perverts the conjugal act, the intimate giving of spouses to each other. It does grave injury to the dignity of its participants (actors, vendors, the public), since each one becomes an object of base pleasure and illicit profit for others. It immerses all who are involved in the illusion of a fantasy world. It is a grave offense. (n. 2354)

It's not just the occasion of sin, but also serious sin in itself because it degrades sex and all persons involved.

Practical Application

So what does this mean in actual practice? First, since men usually become aroused more quickly than women, a woman must be concerned about how her partner is reacting, not just how she herself is reacting. If he becomes less gentle and more urgent in his embrace or goodnight kiss, it's quite certain that he has gone beyond the threshold of affection. This is the time for either or both to pull back, while saying something complimentary. Why the compliment? To deflect the sin without harming the ego. He (or she) could say something like, "You're very precious to me," or "You're the greatest," before leaving for the night.

A classic question among singles concerns the morality of "French" or tongue kissing. Is it acceptable? Briefly, no. Some women have told me they can do this without getting aroused, and I believe them. But who are they going to kiss? It's hard to imagine a normal male who would not be sent half-way to the moon with a French kiss. Women are responsible for what they do to the man, as well as what they do to themselves.

One eighth-grader told me, "Father, I can French kiss without getting aroused." I replied, "I think you must be doing it wrong." It might be possible for a male to de-sensitize himself by constant practice, but the de-sensitizing process itself would be harmful to his soul, and perhaps to his social life as well.

Finally, what if someone gets aroused by affection alone? It would seem that by the principle of double effect, a certain amount of this may be okay. The key is not to will the arousal directly in itself. However, any long-term sharing of affection that results in arousal should be avoided, since the longer the arousal continues, the more likely it is that the will is going to embrace it.

Another issue here that often gets overlooked is the situation of a man and woman sitting on the couch and kissing "just affectionately" for some time. Aside from the temptation to fall into sexual sin, there is a problem with this. The whole purpose of courtship is to get to know the other person in order to see if you should get married. Kissing for a long period of time is not going to help with that process. It's usually done because it's enjoyable, not for interpersonal discovery. So even if there were no arousal in long-term kissing (which itself might be a medical phenomenon), it's counterproductive for true courtship. Long-term kissing is, at best, a sin against prudence.

Summing It Up

In summary, the Scriptures clearly proclaim the serious sinfulness of pre-marital sex. The Church draws the reasonable conclusion that all activity aimed at sexual arousal outside of marriage is seriously immoral. Sex is such a deeply profound word of committed love, that it, and its preparation, belong only in a committed relationship, namely marriage.

A chaste courtship is a very tall order for the twenty-first century, but not nearly as tall an order as the gospel, of which this is an essential part. Before we go into more detail on how to live this out, let's look at why, based on the nature of human existence, this is the way to true happiness.

Chapter Four

Why a Chaste, Christian Courtship?

One of the greatest religious problems in the twenty-first century is the confusion about moral issues. Many Christians believe that moral norms are external constraints placed by God to see if we will obey him. In other words, living immorally might bring us more happiness, but since God doesn't approve, we should not do it. Nothing could be further from the truth. The moral law is the Creator's operating instructions, the blueprint for our real happiness. It is tailored to our nature as persons, and ordered to our fulfillment as complex, rational, feeling persons.

Imagine, if you will, a world in which men and women really lived God's moral code with regard to sexuality. There would be no illegitimate children, very little venereal disease, much less lying, women would have far more control of their own lives, men would begin to relate to women as persons rather than as sex objects. The entertainment media would have to portray women as persons as well, not playthings. What a decent world that would be.

The best source for information about what is right and wrong is certainly the word of God and his Church. Nonetheless, it might help us to understand our moral teaching if we can see the wisdom of God's teaching on chastity in light of the human condition.

Applying the Four Loves

Given the four different dynamics of love we discussed earlier, it is clear why pre-marital sexual activity is wrong. First of all, the courtship of a man and woman is meant to be a time to develop the habits of divine love, of friendship, and of affection in their relationship, so that in marriage when sexual intimacy comes into play, selfishness will not take over. Anything pleasurable can easily lead to selfishness, and this is certainly the case with sex. Christianity is designed to eliminate selfishness and promote true self-giving (divine) love.

Engaging in any sexual activity, before the marriage commitment will often dull the appetite for the less exciting, more fundamental loves: *agape*, friendship, and affection. The development of these "quieter" loves may well be stunted. Some couples even find after a few years that they have so little in common besides sex they have no basis for friendship. This was not apparent during the courtship since the physical and emotional elements were so prominent.

Those who live together before marriage fail to understand the unique sort of bonding which occurs when people do not live together. Couples are forced to relate at the personal level, not the physical, in a true Christian courtship. They have to talk a great deal. They have to share the deep longings of their hearts and their most private dreams. These are the things that makes for a good marriage, not simply keeping or "playing" house.

Living together before marriage can become quite mundane, especially if there is no understanding of intimate, personal sharing. When a couple has developed a habit of sharing personal feelings and hopes before they marry, they are unlikely to fall into the boring routine of being roommates. To be sure, the advent of children can also lift parents out of this boredom and help them grow in friendship.

In any event, getting to know someone well is the main purpose of courtship, and living together does not guarantee that. Perhaps the unfulfilled presumption that living together will automatically provide personal intimacy is why the divorce rate is about 50 percent higher among those who have lived together before marriage than those who have not.[1]

Some argue for living together by saying, "You wouldn't buy a car without trying it, would you?" No, but a car is an object for which you shop around to find the cheapest price. After you buy it, you use it for some years and then trade it in for a new one. Is that the way people should be treated? Is this the way you want to be treated?

The Christian view of sex as expressed in *Gaudium et spes* is that the conjugal act "signifies and fosters the mutual self-donation by which spouses enrich each other with a joyful and a ready mind." It symbolizes a total self-donation, a love which is fruitful, which doesn't wish to end in itself, but to go beyond a selfish *egoisme à deux* as the French put it, to new life.

The Thought of Pope John Paul II

Pope John Paul II has written some excellent things on chastity, including his pre-papal *Love and Responsibility* and his "Theology of The Body," which he gave as a series of talks at his Wednesday audiences from 1979 to 1984.

The Holy Father identifies three stages in the human condition:

1. Before Original Sin
2. After Original Sin
3. After the redemptive death of Jesus

Before the fall into Original Sin, humanity had what the Pope called in *Original Unity* the "fullness of vision, by which the 'pure' value of humanity as male and female, the 'pure' value of the body and of sex is manifested. . . . They see and know each other, in fact, with all the peace of the interior gaze, which creates precisely the fullness of the intimacy of persons." Thus, with this "interior gaze" the man and woman can see not just a body, but a person, with all his or her values, interior and exterior.

After the fall into Original Sin, things changed dramatically. Adam said, "I was afraid, because I was naked; and I hid myself" (Genesis 3:10). The Pope comments on this in *Blessed are the Pure of Heart*:

> Man loses, in a way, the original certainty of the "image of God," expressed in his body. He also loses to some extent the sense of his right to participate in the perception of the world, which he enjoyed in the mystery of creation. This right had its foundation in man's inner self, in the fact that he himself participated in the divine vision of the world and of his own humanity; which gave him deep peace and joy in living the truth and value of his own body. . . .

Man has lost the "interior gaze" he had in original innocence, in which he was able to see beyond exterior appearances to the whole person, which the body expressed.

It is as if prior to the Fall, humanity saw others in their totality, in "living color." After the Fall, that picture changes, so that only the physical values are seen in color, and the interior, or spiritual, values appear in black and white. The physical values, which are sexual values, predominate.

In place of the "interior gaze" is the superficial vision of a body, and the superficial response to that body.

John Paul also comments on Matthew 5:28: ". . . if a man looks at a woman lustfully he has already committed adultery with her in his heart." These words, he says, constitute not just an accusation, but "an appeal to the heart." In the light of redemption, he goes on to say:

> Man must feel called to rediscover, nay more, realize the nuptial meaning of the body and to express in this way the interior freedom of the gift, that is, of that spiritual state and that spiritual power which are derived from mastery of the lust of the flesh.
>
> Christ's words bear witness that the original power (therefore also the grace) of the mystery of creation becomes for each of them power (that is, grace) of the mystery of redemption.

He adds that Christ does not invite man back to the state of original innocence, but to live as the "new man" of redemption, in purity of heart, in perfection. Nonetheless, in the behavioral pattern, "of the redemption of the body, the original ethos of creation will have to be taken up again." Man re-establishes, "with an even deeper power and firmness . . . the value of the nuptial meaning of the body, by. . . which the Creator . . . has written in the heart of both, the gift of communion." Man becomes free again to love, not to use,[2] because by grace, he has recovered the "fullness of vision" he had in the beginning.

Pope John Paul describes chastity in its positive sense in *Love and Responsibility*:

The essence of chastity consists in quickness to affirm the value of the person in every situation, and in raising to the personal level all reactions to the value of "the body and sex." This requires a special interior, spiritual effort, for affirmation of the value of the person can only be the product of the spirit, but this effort is above all positive and creative "from within," not negative and destructive. It is not a matter of summarily "annihilating" the value "body and sex" in the conscious mind by pushing reactions to them down into the subconscious, but of sustained long term integration; the value of "body and sex" must be grounded and implanted in the value of the person.

In his redeemed state, a man can relate to a woman as a person,[3] not just a body, an object of use.

This fits in with our analysis of the four loves. Friendship, affection, and especially divine love (*agape*) are person-affirming loves, whereas sexual activity without these loves having become an ingrained habit, and without the commitment sex implies, tends to de-personalize the other. It makes this other person an object *for* me rather than one united *to* me in love. Only when a person relates to a partner as a person, rather than an object, will there be the experience the joy of a deep, enriching love.

Dignity of Women[4]

A young woman once told me she had slept with her boyfriend. When she seemed unimpressed with the Scriptural prohibitions against premarital sex, I told her, "You know, you're his slave." Her eyes widened and she replied, "You're right. He's not committed, but I am. I don't want to go out and find someone else after we've done this, but he would. No more sex!" Another woman was afraid to tell her "Catholic" boyfriend that she couldn't sleep with him anymore. She was afraid he might break up with her. Eventually she told him, and he didn't break up. After a few more dates, however, she decided she really didn't love him, so she broke up with him! When they were sleeping together, she couldn't see how bad the relationship was because she was trying so hard to save it. When she stepped back and was able to look at it objectively, she saw how unhappy she was.

All of this simply points to something the wise have known for centuries: women have the most to lose in pre-marital sex. In modern terms, the sexual revolution has been bad for everyone, but women have gotten the worst of it.

Why was the sexual revolution so bad for women? When a woman has sex with a man she bonds with him and feels committed to him because she is more integrated than the man. A man does not necessarily feel committed when he has sex. What often follows, then, is a relationship in which one person is committed, and the other is not. The woman tends to put up with his bad behavior because she does not want to go out and find someone else. The man, if he gives in to his lower nature, tends to be more and more casual about the way he treats her, because he discovers she'll accept it. The result is often bad treatment for women before marriage, and if there is a marriage, the same bad treatment or worse after marriage.

In the early 60's women began to agree more and more to men's immoral requests and thus began to be treated worse. By the early 70's many women had had enough and the feminist revolution began in earnest. The leaders did a marvelous job of identifying the problem, but their solution was worse than the problem. They decided that women could be just like men, asking men out if they wanted, paying for dates if they chose and engaging in lots of sex, as long as they could have abortions to cover their mistakes.

Unfortunately, women can't enjoy casual sex without doing violence to their natures. And, certainly not abortion. This trend made the breach between the sexes even deeper. The divorce rate has doubled since 1960[5]. And, some estimates claim that as many as 50 percent of the members of the National Organization for Women are lesbians. Clearly, NOW's version of feminism isn't working.

Others are starting to come forward with the same conclusion. Danielle Chrittendon writes in *What Our Mothers Didn't Tell Us: Why Happiness Eludes the Modern Woman*:

> . . . the woman who comes of age today quickly discovers that she enjoys a . . . guarantee of 'sexual equality': the right to make love to a man and never see him again; the right to be insulted and demeaned if she refuses a man's advances; the right to catch a sexually transmitted disease, that might, as a bonus, leave her infertile; the right to an abortion when things go wrong, or, as it may be, the right to bear a child out of wedlock. Indeed, in all the promises made to us about our ability to achieve freedom and independence as women, the promise of sexual emancipation may have been the most illusory."

In *A Return to Modesty* Wendy Shallit points out "The peculiar way our culture tries to prevent young women from seeking more than 'just sex,' the way it attempts to rid us of our romantic hopes or, variously, our embarrassment and our 'hang-ups,' is a misguided effort. It is, I will argue, no less than an attempt to cure woman-hood itself, and in many cases it has actually put us in danger." And, argue she does, quite effectively, using articles written by the liberationists themselves in *Cosmopolitan*, *Elle*, and *Mademoiselle*. Columnist Mona Charen opined some time back that the absti-nence program, *Best Friends*, which helps high school girls post-pone sex, turn down drugs and alcohol, and develop real self-esteem, has given back to these girls their femininity.

The point is, women can regain their feminine dignity by living Christian chastity, and helping both themselves and their men to be saved. If men won't raise the culture to a Christian level (as indeed they should) then women can do it, as they have through-out the centuries. Bishop Fulton J. Sheen had great insight when he said that the level of civilization of any society is always deter-mined by the women. If women refuse to give in to premarital sex, and insist that men treat them well before and in marriage, they will raise up the level of the whole culture.

Men and Chastity

Men have a good deal to gain from chastity, besides saving their souls (as if that weren't enough!), although for them the benefits are subtler. By committing to chastity and sticking to it, men build up their women more, and allow them to be confident, alluring and mysterious. So often men who have the superior attitude which accompanies pre-marital sex are greatly disappointed to find their wives have become mousy little women. They seldom realize that they helped create this woman!

By honoring the virtue of their women, men help them to be real persons, with real minds, and real wills, not the willful, angry woman who has rebelled against the bad treatment that so often accompanies unchaste courtships. The woman given over to the Lord is at peace with her identity, her husband, and the world. Additionally, a chaste man can live in peace with his appetites, and avoid the selfishness which accompanies sexual license. He will be able to transmit the faith to his children in its entirety, because he has lived it. He will know the difficulties because he has faced them himself, and overcome them. Blessed the children of such a father!

Premarital Sex and Divorce

The correlation between having premarital sex and divorce is well known. According to a 1992 study published by the University of Chicago, men who have had premarital sex are 63 percent more likely to get divorced than if they had not. Women are 76 percent more likely to divorce if they have had premarital sex.[6]

Sometimes it is argued that the values of those who do not have premarital sex are likely to be more traditional and therefore more suited to permanence in marriage. True. We are not encouraging people to just avoid premarital sex while holding on to worldly values. What is being proposed is nothing short of conversion to Christ and his entire way of life.

Are Christians Too Concerned With Sex?

The world asks why Christians are so concerned about sex. What's the big deal? In fact, the world is far more concerned about sex than Christians are. We do, however have a much more reverent attitude toward sex than does the world.

It is difficult to dialog with the world on this subject, since the world has adopted the dogma of pansexualism. The world has convinced itself that everyone should have sex with whomever and whenever he/she wishes, with few exceptions. That unrestrained sex may produce babies is solved by contraception and, if necessary, abortion.

But, in a moment of candor, many would admit that sex is more than a plaything, and people are more than objects of pleasure. Sex has a deep effect on the participants. Sex is a profound language of love which symbolizes an intimate union. It is a love which overflows into the drawing forth of new life from the hand of the Creator. In no way is it superficial or peripheral, but part of the core which involves the whole person. One's sexuality might be called his aesthetic core, the place where a person is beautiful, poetic, and artistic.

Sex is also the act in which man "expresses and perfects" his love for his spouse. Every time a man has sex with his spouse he is saying (whether truthfully or not) "I am committed to you for life; I give myself *totally* to you. I love no one else in this way and my love for you is so total that I wish to have that love overflow generously into new life, which will in turn be a symbol of our love forever."[7] This is the innate, intrinsic meaning of sex, which makes it both beautiful and sublime.

When sex is misused, it seems there is an inevitable sadness, which is at best a wistfulness and at worst a self-alienation. The idealist within rails at the beautiful symphony which should be inside, but which has been ruined by giving in to an appetite for pleasure. Clearly this is apparent when one thinks of the most terrible expletive one can shout at another. That awful expression which begins with "f" signifies "I wish you all the self-alienation that comes *from unlawful carnal knowledge.*" This is an implicit acknowledgment of the fact that sex is sacred and that its misuse is tragic.

Virtually every human heart understands that sex is not, and should not be treated as trifling. Sex is not merely a recreational activity. "Hooking up," the practice of meeting someone and having sex, and never seeing each other again, was one of the saddest cultural fads ever to come along.

Summing It Up

Unchaste behavior will not bring happiness because it short-circuits the richer, quieter, yet more fundamental loves such as *agape*, friendship and affection. When a man courts a woman chastely, he discovers the profundity of her personhood, which is deeply fulfilling. When a woman insists on chastity, she gains an equal footing in the relationship, rather than the "slavery" of feeling bound to a man who is not bound to her because they have had sex. The man who insists on a chaste courtship will build confidence in his woman, make her more attractive, and help her become a good model for his children. By courting chastely, both the man and woman will avoid the sadness of trivializing sex.

True Christianity cannot accept the lie of the world, no matter how prevalent it may be. As Christians we must uphold the truth about sex and the truth about humanity. Sex is good, beautiful, and reserved for marriage. And, we can, with the help of God, live the dignity of chastity.

Endnotes

1. See Popenoe and Whitehead's, "Should We Live Together?" at http://marriage.rutgers.edu.

2. The Holy Father put forth the "personalist norm" as "The person is a good toward which the only proper and adequate attitude is love." Stated negatively: "The person is the kind of good which does not admit of use, and cannot be treated as an object of use, and as such the means to an end." (Karol Wojtyla, *Love and Responsibility*, p. 41.)

3. Is *eros* stronger when you relate to the whole person? Absolutely! Is this dangerous? Yes, without the transforming power of agapaic love. *Agape* enables you to channel this stronger desire into service, rather than a grasping possession of the beloved.

4. This section is excerpted from an article published in *Laywitness* Magazine in July 2000, entitled "Women: The Key to Cultural Renewal."

5. Bridget Maher, *The Family Portrait*, Washington, DC: The Family Research Council, 2002.

6. Edward O. Laumann, et al. *The Social Organization of Sexuality: Sexual Practices in the United States* (Chicago: U. of Chicago Press, 1994. This is "regarded as the most authoritative and best designed recent survey on sex." As cited in Bridget Maher's *The Family Portrait*, Washington, DC: The Family Research Council, 2002, p. 63.

7. This is not to say that every sex act must be for the purpose of having children, but it should symbolize conjugal love, which itself should be open to new life.

Chapter Five

Living a Christian Courtship

It is possible to really have a Christian courtship in the twenty-first century. It is possible to live gospel chastity without a great struggle every day. It is possible to have a real Christian courtship, even if you haven't in the past.

To begin with, let's look at the virtue of chastity. According to Thomas Aquinas and Aristotle, chastity is *the habitual moderation of the sexual appetite in accord with right reason.* In other words, it's bringing the sexual appetite consistently under reason.[1]

It is not just the regulation of behavior, which would be self-control, but of the very desires that lead to sexual behavior. Note too, the norm is "right" reason, i.e., reason in conformity with God's eternal law, not merely worldly reason, which views any sex which avoids unwanted pregnancy or disease as reasonable.

How to Live Chastely

How do you develop the *virtue* of chastity so that you habitually live without a struggle, or, as Thomas Aquinas put it, "joyfully, easily and promptly"?

As a fruit of the Holy Spirit, chastity is not something you can arrive at without considerable prayer and effort. The fruits of a tree appear after the leaves and blossoms, and so it is with the Holy Spirit's fruits. They require a good deal of cultivation through God's grace. To begin to live chastely requires a strong spiritual life. Fifteen minutes of meditation daily plus frequent Mass and reception of the sacraments would seem essential to anyone hoping to live out this virtue.

Convincing the Self

Besides Mass and the sacraments, you can employ several other methods to effectively use the grace received from spiritual exercises to develop chastity. Begin by observing with Aristotle and Thomas Aquinas that the sexual appetite seems to have a life of its own, and it listens not only to reason, but to the senses and the imagination as well. If I want to raise my hand, I tell it to move, and it moves. But if my sexual appetite is attracted to something illicit, I must do more than tell it, "Forget it." The sexual appetite can be very persistent.

As St. Paul says:

> For I do not do the good I want, but the evil I do not want is what I do. . . For I delight in the law of God, in my inmost self, but I see in my members another law at war with the law of my mind and making me captive to the law of sin which dwells in my members. Wretched man that I am!" (Romans 7:19, 23, 24.)

Thus, you must find a way to "convince" your sexual appetite to obey reason and not the senses or the imagination.

Taming the Senses and Tempering the Imagination

Since the appetite listens to the senses, you must be careful about what you look at or watch. Viewing sexually explicit movies or pornography or even focusing on provocatively dressed members of the opposite sex is poison if you are seeking chastity. The worst of these is viewing pornographic web sites or materials, since pornography depicts sex as merely recreational and women (or men) as mere objects of enjoyment.

You can hardly expect to keep from sexual sins if you are constantly viewing sexually explicit images. Pornography is the devil's cocaine for the mind.

The imagination is another potential danger area. When you become aware of an impure thought, immediately try to substitute another wholesome thought, such as a ball game,[2] or a beautiful sunset, etc. Also, take the advice of St. John Vianney to make a sign of the cross to drive away the temptation or say the name of Jesus repeatedly in your heart as advised by St. Catherine of Siena. An uninvited impure thought is not sinful, but once you will its continuation, sin enters in. As Jesus pointed out, you can sin seriously in the heart as well as the body.

The Values of Chastity

Since competing voices vie for the control of the sexual appetite, it doesn't work for reason to deal with the appetite "despotically," in other words simply saying "no" to the appetite's appeal, and, then when it asks why not, replying, "because I said no." If this is done, Pope John Paul points out in *Love and Responsibility*, the appetite will be repressed into the unconscious where it will wait for a chance to "explode." In a moment of weakness the appetite will indeed explode with an outburst of sexual activity. We see this in the person who contains himself/herself for several weeks but then goes on a spree, and repeats this cycle over and over.

The intellect must deal "politically" with the appetite, setting forth the values which will be gained by living chastity, to make up for the value of the sexual pleasure which is sacrificed. One must, in a sense, convince the appetite that it will not make your entire being happy to give in to it. You must hammer away with reason to convert your heart to the truth. It's not enough to know what is right and wrong. To survive chastely in this world, you must be completely convinced mind and heart of the benefits of chastity.

What are some of the benefits of a chaste life you can remind yourself about so as to alleviate any interior resentment and find peace? First and foremost is the most precious gift we have as Christians: our personal love relationship with Jesus Christ. To freely and knowingly violate chastity is to destroy that relationship with the Lord, a relationship which is our source of happiness and our only way to salvation. To destroy that is a huge price to pay for a few moments of pleasure.

Another value retained by opting for chastity is that of upholding the sacredness of sex. Sex is so sacred that it belongs only in marriage. By living chastely you avoid trivializing sex as something merely recreational, so that when you do participate in it within marriage, you will experience its sublime dignity and transcendence.

A further value is that by opting for chastity, you will be living up to your own human dignity as a person created in the image and likeness of God. As such, you are empowered to live by reason, rather than merely be controlled by your urges and impulses (as are animals). In living according to reason, you fulfill your noble dignity as a person made in God's image.

By refraining from sexual activity, you are also able to uphold the value of the other person as a whole, rather than fall into the tendency to see the other as merely an object of enjoyment. The value of sex is just one treasure in a rich storehouse of values a person has, a profoundly precious one to be sure, but only one of many. To participate in sex before marriage gives rise to the natural tendency, particularly in men, to look at the woman as primarily an object of enjoyment, rather than as a person who is his equal and worthy of love, and not mere use.

A further value is the importance of developing the most important types of love during courtship. Self-giving love (*agape*), friendship and affection are the loves that hold a marriage together. They should be developed into habits while dating so that by the time the marriage begins, and sexual relations are meant to come into play, these other, less exciting but more fundamental loves will be almost second nature.

Couples who share sex together before marriage most likely do not develop these more selfless loves as habits. Selfishness tends to creep in, as it so often does with anything so pleasurable as sex. Couples refraining from sex before marriage are far more likely to be willing to serve each other in *agape* and to be able to express their love by affection without always having to move into sex. Additionally, they are more likely to develop the common interests that lie at the heart of every good friendship. In fact, sexual involvement before marriage can hide the fatal flaw of a fundamental lack of friendship, which is so essential to a good marriage.

By constantly reminding yourself of these values you can, in a sense, graft reason onto your appetite, to the point that the appetite in time will agree to participate in reason. The values of chastity must be "objectivized" and internalized, as Pope John Paul says, so that the will is constantly "confronted by a value which fully explains the necessity for containing impulses aroused by carnal desire and sensuality. Only as this value takes possession of the mind and will does the will become calm and free itself from a characteristic sense of loss." In other words you repeatedly recall the truth about sex and your own happiness, until the appetite in a sense "gives up," and surrenders to reason. Only when this happens will the appetite be in conformity with the mind, and you will arrive at the peace of chastity.

Another way of putting this is to say that it's not enough to convert your mind; you have to convert your heart as well. A sign of an unconverted heart is a person theoretically wanting to live chastely, but who does nothing to avoid the dangers of sins against chastity. Others, while accepting the Church's teaching on sex, either out of boredom or attachment to the thrill of temptation, insist on at least flirting with illicit sex. This is particularly insidious. Take for example, a couple who start prolonged kissing, even though this has led to serious sins before or a case in which one person will invite the other to stay the night, claiming "nothing is going to happen!" These couples have already sinned seriously against love and prudence by deliberately and needlessly placing themselves in temptation. If you struggle with chastity, you must remind yourself of the values to be gained by a chaste life several times a day if necessary, regardless of whether you are tempted at the moment or not. In the long run, we are more attracted to the truth than to sensual pleasures. This is why, if we repeat the truth often enough, we can convert even our own wild sexual appetite.

Self-Control as the 'Parent'

Self-control must serve as a parent to the sexual appetite until it is trained, but self-control is not a full-fledged virtue in itself since it involves a constant battle. Chastity, on the other hand, is a true virtue, since it wins the appetite over to reason, thereby eliminating the battle. With chastity the person has head and heart united in pursuing the more noble values of a relationship with the Lord, the truth about the sacredness of sex, and loving another as a human person in his/her dignity.

One of the great destroyers of self-control is excessive drinking. Many people get into terrible trouble due to alcohol abuse. If you hope to live the virtue of chastity, you should resolve never to take more than one drink in an evening. I made a resolution never to drink at all while I was in college which proved to be a huge blessing. While you may not make the same decision, be very careful of alcohol and, of course, drugs. They can be life-destroyers. No real Christian would play with these things knowing how they shatter self-control. You need self-control if you hope to obtain the peace of chastity.

Dealing With the World

But your own life isn't all you must think about. You must also deal with an oversexed world. To do this, you have to know what you want, and stick to it. If you don't, you will get dragged down into the mess the world has created for dating.

The first thing is to establish how you are going to share affection in courtship. Earlier we proposed a whole array of ways to share affection. Sticking to that agenda for sharing affection will certainly enable you to have a chaste courtship. The question is, how do you get this across to someone right from the start?

It begins before you ever agree to a courtship with what I call friendship dating. With this approach, you just get together as friends once a week or so, for one to three months with no kissing. A chaste hug, yes, but no romantic words, no hand-holding, no commitment. If your partner accepts that, you have a good start. You can't take for granted that the person you've been friendship dating will understand the affection-only program. Sometimes couples will go through this early part of the routine just fine. But once they get into a courtship, they go wild. So you have to make it clear what you want.

Let's imagine a couple in which the girl wants to have a chaste approach to the physical side of courtship. If the guy is confused, she might explain gently that means, "We only share affection — hugs, touches, holding hands. Kisses are very tender, and only for saying goodnight. No Hollywood kisses."

If he hesitates, she should simply say, "Why don't you think about it. No hurry." If he makes it clear he will not agree, then she can politely say, "Okay. It's good we had this discussion before we got started. I've really enjoyed your friendship." It is absolutely crucial that she be very firm at this point. Polite, gracious, but firm. If the guy walks, he walks. She will have saved herself from a long struggle for chastity, and perhaps a bad marriage.

If the roles are reversed and he is into the program and wants to bring her on board, he can simply say something like, "I would propose that we just share affection on dates. Are you okay with that?" If she agrees, he can continue, "I propose that we just stick to affection, that is, hugs, touches, holding hands. Kisses would be only for saying goodnight. Will that be acceptable to you?" If she balks, and indicates she wants lots more physical activity, he's the one to walk.

If you compromise your position from the start, you'll quickly slide into the typical oversexed courtship. Even if you refrain from sexual intercourse, there'll be lots of foreplay which will destroy the whole program. Now is the time to be certain, and strong.

Isn't it a bit awkward to have to explain this from the very start of the courtship? It is, but it's much better to do that early rather than have to go through all this after an unfortunate incident. I strongly recommend that you make things clear from the first. Everyone will know exactly where he stands.

Is Accommodation Enough?

Often it's the man who accommodates himself to the woman's ethic, but not always. In any case, accommodation is really not enough. The one who is living chastely only because he or she is dating a convinced Christian is not in the state of grace. He or she must believe the truth of the gospel and try to live it to be a follower of Christ. The one who thinks he or she is virtuous just because they are going along with the chastity program is in a dream world. Following Christ means having the gospel within you, not following some external constraint. Of course, such a person is far more virtuous than one who refuses to go along with chastity.

But it's not enough. The converted one, let's say the woman for the sake of argument, should remind him gently, "It's great that you are going along with me on this, but really, that's not enough. You need to be convinced that this is what Jesus wants and that you want to live this way for him. God forbid you should ever get in an accident and die before you converted on this. I realize it may take some time, but I hope you'll think about it. The stakes are high."

Neither men nor women have an excuse when it comes to the acceptance of gospel morality. Both have a serious obligation to study it, to know it, to accept it, and to then convert their own heart to really embrace it with every fiber of their being.

One woman told me she felt sorry for her fiancé because he found it so difficult when she insisted they be chaste. She shouldn't have felt sorry for reigning him in, but for the fact that he never had learned the happiness that comes from personally embracing gospel chastity.

Is Reform Possible?

When discussing chastity, a question which often arises: "Do you think it is possible for someone who has made mistakes in the past to begin to live chastely and do it successfully?"

The answer is "Yes, absolutely!" The devil would have us think, "You can never live chastely now, not after what you have done. And you can certainly never encourage others to do so, you hypocrite!" Another flimsy lie from the father of lies. Who better to witness about the sadness of a sex-addicted life than one who has been freed from that slavery and has tasted the freedom of living for Christ? Grace really does make you a "new creation in Christ" (2 Corinthians 5:17). So, to anyone who asks that question, the answer is "Yes, you can live chastely. And, you can become a *saint* as well." Just think of St. Augustine, who lived with his mistress for fourteen years before turning away from his "cruel slavery to lust" and found peace and happiness in the Lord Jesus as well as sainthood! There have been others such as St. Margaret of Cortona and St. John of God. Some of the best defenders of chastity have been those who were its greatest violators in the past.

Grace

As we have mentioned before, you cannot live chastely without grace, and a good deal of it. This is why a number of young single Catholics are forming groups to support each other, not only in living chaste lives, but more fundamentally in having a strong spiritual life. Many are praying the Rosary daily, getting to Mass most weekdays as well as Sunday, and reading spiritual books. Some are making a holy hour or half-hour each day before the Blessed Sacrament. They are not only able to live chastely but they are discovering the joy of having a close, personal relationship with Jesus Christ. They have learned, as did St. Augustine, "Our hearts are restless until they rest in him."

No Compromises

You must have a strong commitment to be faithful to God and his will when you are courting. So often, when you compromise on a small thing, it's the beginning of a big collapse. Every compromise you make will harm your friendship with your sweetheart. You have to be convinced that doing things God's way will always bring you more happiness, as indeed it will. Ask yourself, "What would Jesus do? What would Mary do?" If you have a good prayer life, you will have the grace to do what they would do.

Ask the Lord in prayer specifically to help you always live chastely. Especially ask for this virtue right after receiving Holy Communion. This is our most intimate time with the Lord, and the best time to seek his help. As Teresa of Ávila said, "After communion let us be careful not to lose so good an opportunity of negotiating with God. His Divine Majesty is not accustomed to pay badly for his lodging if he meets with a good reception." As the

Catechism says: "Those who are engaged to marry are called to live chastity in continence. They should see in this time of testing a discovery of mutual respect, an apprenticeship in fidelity, and the hope of receiving one another from God . . . (n. 2350). The Church wants you to receive each other from God, not from the world.

Practical Matters

One thing that makes living chastely difficult is having a boring life. A surprisingly large number of people are struggling with chastity because they don't have enough fun. I always encourage people coming to me for spiritual direction to do something enjoyable every week. You have to have something to look forward to each week whether it's playing a sport such as tennis, racquetball, sailing, basketball; playing cards; reading a fascinating book; watching a great video; or whatever interests you. We all have psyches that need to be nourished. To be bored with life is to become a prime candidate for temptation and sin. This boredom with life is also one of the reasons why people stay up too late at night. When it's time to retire, they say to themselves subconsciously, "Is that all there is to this day? Perhaps if I extend the day another hour or two, I'll have some fun."

When you are bored with life, you become desperate for a little stimulation, and you will be far more likely to fall into the trap of pornography, or other sexual addictions, which can make you oversexed when dating. Leading a boring life because you haven't planned some fun in your life can not only lead to sexual addiction, it can lead to real depression. In turn, you become so down you don't have the energy to plan some fun. A vicious circle thus begins. To counter it, schedule some good, clean, healthy, enjoyable activities weekly. Your life will become much more balanced, and you won't be desperate for sexual stimulation or a destructive love!

Summing It Up

The first step toward chastity is to convert your appetite and to win your heart over to the truth about sexuality and the happiness chastity brings. This involves a real conversion of the heart by convincing it of the values it will gain by refraining from immoral sexual activity — values such as being in the state of grace; upholding the sacredness of sex; living by reason instead of by urges as do animals; treating your sweetheart as a person worthy of love instead of falling into the tendency of seeing him or her as an object of use; and the value of building the more fundamental loves such as friendship, affection, and *agape* in courtship so that they will become habits by the time you marry. Once you convince yourself, you may have to convince your girlfriend or boyfriend. This is best done by simply proposing the affection-only program, and holding firmly to it. Do what is right, and let the chips fall where they may. You won't regret it.

Couples who have courted this way have found it truly refreshing, and a true enhancement to human dignity, especially for the woman. Moreover, this kind of courtship makes a great foundation for a healthy marriage.

As John Paul II says in *Love and Responsibility*, "Chastity is a difficult, long-term matter; one must wait patiently for it to bear fruit, for the happiness of loving kindness which it must bring. But at the same time, chastity is the sure way to happiness." Chastity may not be easy in our oversexed society, but with the grace that comes through the Mass, the sacraments and prayer, it *is* possible.

Remember, what we are ultimately seeking is not chastity for its own sake, but the Kingdom. Chastity is very important, but it is not the most important thing. The most important thing is having a prayer life, a sacramental life, a life of worship; in short, a love relationship with God that is so strong and so intimate that it will make living chastely easy.

Endnotes

1. As we saw earlier, the *Catechism of the Catholic Church* teaches in a less technical way, "Chastity means the successful integration of sexuality within the person and thus the inner unity of man in his bodily and spiritual being . . ." (n. 2337).

2. I told a man in confession once to think about a Washington Redskins football game when he was tempted. Unfortunately, it was a down year, and he replied, "Father, I can't do that. It's too depressing!"

Chapter Six

A Modesty Proposal[1]

A chastity program simply cannot work without the virtue of modesty of dress in both men and women. Although we don't often think of it, men must be modest, too. Tiny bathing suits, skin-tight trousers, and T-shirts with the arms cut away deep into the center of the shirt would be examples of immodest dress for men, as well as something that flies in the face of true Christianity. However, as St. Teresa of Avila wrote in her autobiography, ". . . women are obliged to modesty more than men." Thus, we will focus mostly on issues of women's modesty.

Let me share a story with you. One evening, a member of our Catholic single women's group was trying to decide what to wear to a wedding. She called her father and asked him what he thought. He said, "Well, you have nice legs, why not wear something short?"

So, she wore something short . . . and created quite a stir. It was not her happiest moment.

After that we began to discuss modesty and she started to wear more demure outfits. Later, she told me she had attended one party and got more attention in her modest clothing than others did in their revealing wear!

Since women are more integrated than men, and see the whole person, they are often unaware of how men are looking at them. Pope John Paul II pointed this out *in Love and Responsibility*:

> Since sensuality, which is oriented towards "the body as an object of enjoyment" is in general stronger and more important in men, modesty and shame — the tendency to conceal sexual values specifically connected with the body — must be more pronounced in girls and women.

Yet, since the woman is not nearly as "physical" in her attraction as the man is, she often does not feel the need for modesty. John Paul concludes, then, that "The evolution of modesty in woman requires some initial insight into the male psychology." Women often are aware that men are attracted to them physically, but they seldom have even the remotest idea of the intensity of that attraction. When a woman sees a good-looking man, she may think, "Nice." When a man sees a good-looking woman, his response is much more powerful.

Many young men who believe in chastity, even those who try hard to live it, have never thought about modest dress in women. Some are perfectly willing to visually exploit a woman in a tight, short skirt, or a bikini, though not physically. Often as they begin to think about the root causes of lust, they start to recognize the negative effect this has on them. One man who has taken the time to reflect on just what is happening when men face a sexily dressed woman is Fr. David Knight. In *The Good News About Sex*, he writes:

> I think we would have to be deliberately naive in this age of psychological sophistication to ignore the fact that cer-

tain visual stimuli are objectively and normally provocative to the sex drive of the ordinary male. We might close our eyes to this, but the merchants don't. And the fortunes they make by putting their theories into practice prove they know what they are doing . . . Whether the women and girls of our culture know or do not know what is going on, they lose by it all the same. . . . In the measure that a particular style of dress is consciously and deliberately provocative — whether the deliberate intent is on the part of the designer, or the wearer, or of both — this way of dressing must be recognized as a mild form of reverse rape by which a person arouses un-solicited sexual desire in another person who may not want to be aroused. Whenever this happens to men (who are more subject to this kind of arousal than women) it always causes some anger, whether recognized or not. . . .

Furthermore, the *Catechism* teaches:

Modesty protects the intimate center of the person. It means refusing to unveil what should remain hidden. It is ordered to chastity to whose sensitivity it bears witness. It guides how one looks at others and behaves toward them in conformity with the dignity of persons and their soli-darity.

Modesty protects the mystery of persons and their love. It encourages patience and moderation in loving relationships; it requires that the conditions for the definitive giving and commitment of man and woman to one another be fulfilled. Modesty is decency. It inspires one's choice of clothing . . . (nn. 2521, 2522).

What's Immodest These Days?

What are some of the most prevalent elements of dress nowadays that cause reactions in men? The most common one is short skirts. Several times I have heard from devout men that they could not believe how short some of the dresses were on women coming into church for daily Mass or prayer. The men saw the women's dress and their devotion as completely contradictory. I had to agree with the men. I am always amazed at the number of prayerful women who never make the religious connection about clothing, i.e., God cares about what we wear. Moreover, decent men care what women wear too.

Dresses or skirts cut way above the knee do affect men sexually, at least in a mild way, but perhaps even more psychologically. That is, their opinion of the woman as a whole is affected. Women wearing longer dresses or skirts often look fashionable, feminine and very appealing to the man who wants a virtuous wife.

Other things which typically stir a certain sexual reaction in men include bare navels, semi-exposed breasts, tight clothes, "sexy hair," and revealing swimsuits. Sometimes women are truly surprised to hear the way men are reacting to them.

One women (who happened to be from California) responded to a talk I gave on modesty by saying, "Are you saying we shouldn't wear bikinis at the beach?"

"Yeah, that's what I'm saying."

"That's kind of extreme, isn't it?"

"Very. Almost as extreme as the Gospel itself."

Several months later I saw her at the beach in a one-piece bathing suit. Her conversion had begun! Four years later she entered a contemplative Carmelite Order. Now *that's* extreme — in the best sense!

Women, do you want to be remembered for your legs? Your navel? Your chest? Your figure? Or, do you want to be remembered for your warmth, your femininity, your personality, your decency, your goodness, your holiness? If a woman over-accentuates her physical values, she will surely drown out her other, more personal, more significant, and more lasting values.

What's a Girl to Do?

Occasionally a woman will say, "If men have a problem with what I wear, that's their problem, not mine. They can just deal with it." This is false for several reasons. First, it's not Christian. Christianity is a community activity. St. Paul teaches us, "Carry one another's burdens and so fulfill the law of Christ" (Galatians 6:2). We are saved in community, not in isolation. Such an attitude hardly fulfills the teaching of Christ, "Love your neighbor as yourself." Love, here, remember, means looking out for the good of the other. And second, it's not just their problem in the long run. The woman who dresses immodestly brings problems on herself. Whenever someone says this, a few women get very offended. They say, "You're into the old 'It's all women's fault' for male aggressiveness." Not so. It's not all women's fault, but women have much to gain from dressing modestly.

Similarly, women who have met with bad behavior from men may react, "Look, you're trying to make me feel responsible for what happened." Not so. A woman bears *some* responsibility for the way men react, but that's a far cry from saying men are justified in their bad behavior because of how women dress. They aren't. But when women dress immodestly, they invite a point of view that women are objects to be used. That is a terrible lie that does all women a grave injustice.

Women who react negatively to a plea for modesty, claiming it only justifies the excessive responses of men, are missing the point. Everyone must face up to his or her own responsibility in transforming our culture into one of Christian decency. In fact, women who dress immodesty often complain that men are all "animals." That's because the wild ones come running while the decent men stay away. The woman who dresses immodestly is selling herself short, saying, in effect, that her best assets are her sexual ones. Unfortunately, when a man sees a sexy woman in the afternoon, he develops an attitude that stays with him into the evening, when he picks up his more modest date. So immodestly dressed women hurt not only themselves, but other women as well.

Second, a good Christian woman has so much going for her, that even if short skirts and other "in" fashions were a benefit — which they aren't — they would be of minimal importance. A woman living in the state of grace has an aura which far exceeds any fashion statement. Christian women sometimes underestimate their inner beauty, perhaps because the fashion designers have such a strong influence and place so much stress on the exterior. As the Scriptures says, ". . . women should adorn themselves with proper clothing, with modesty, and sensibly, not with braiding and gold, or pearls or costly attire, but rather by good deeds, as befits women who profess reverence for God by good works" (Peter 2: 9, 10). In other words, it is by their holiness that women should be attractive, not by their fancy or immodest clothes and jewelry. There is, after all, nothing more attractive than holiness.

Third, women need to ask themselves, "Whom am I trying to please, God or the world?" St. James tells us ". . . whoever wishes to be a friend of the world makes himself an enemy of God" (James 4:4). Consider how the Blessed Mother would dress if she were a

25-year-old single woman today. I would speculate, she would be an example of what St. Francis de Sales describes: "For my part, I would have devout people, whether men or women, always be the best dressed in a group but the least pompous and affected. As the proverb says, I would have them 'adorned with grace, decency and dignity.' "

Some people argue that times have changed and styles are much more revealing today than sixty years ago. For instance, it used to be risqué for a woman to show her legs at the beach. They say that the fashions that are called immodest today may seem quite commonplace twenty or thirty years from now. That may be true, but generally those who are committed to the Lord are not at the cutting edge of revealing styles.

Others may argue, "Well, it's too hot out in the summer." Hot as it may be, there are modest clothes that allow you to be cool. Besides, which is more important, being comfortable or helping people avoid sin — and being treated better as well? Enduring a little heat now could save you lots of heat later on.

The Power of Modesty

A women who is modestly dressed is a woman who doesn't play up to the media, to the designers, or to any man. She's her own woman, or, better yet, she's God's woman. She knows what she wants — decency — and she gets it. There are plenty of modest, chic women who dress fashionably, but not revealingly; women who are in control of their own styles and select decent outfits. These women are also in control of their social lives, and get less pressure for sexual favors than others.

Of course, girls should get the message about modest dress at home, but alas, not all do. Happy the girl with a modesty-conscious mother and father, who are willing to fight the battle for decency.

Why do women dress immodestly? There are, of course, many reasons. Some feel a certain titillation wearing something slinky or revealing; others are driven by fashion; some just want to attract men, and this is a way of doing it.

The fashion argument is weak, given today's eclectic styles. And titillation is hardly a value for the thinking Christian woman. In fact, it's something to be avoided if you wish to draw close to God. The use of immodesty to attract men is an interesting phenomenon. Dressing in a provocative way does give a woman a certain power over men, but it's an expensive power. Like the power from taking drugs or getting drunk, it carries a price. A certain type of man will respond to immodest dress with great energy. But, what type of man is it, and what is his response? The man who delights in sexy women is usually looking for a sexual encounter, and hasn't the slightest inclination toward marriage, at least with the sexy woman. His attitude is certainly not, "I bet she's got a great personality!" or "I bet she'd make a great wife!" It's more like, "I'll bet she's an easy mark."

The Danger of Beauty

Although beauty is a good thing in itself, it too calls for modesty because the extremely attractive woman will receive so many invitations to do evil. The devil is relentless in attempting to recruit beautiful people to his cause.

When a man goes out with a gorgeous woman, he often gets mesmerized by her looks. Even if he thinks she's not the one he wants to marry, he may well hang on for a while until he gets over her beauty. Then he breaks up. Sometimes he hangs on for years before he admits that this is going nowhere.

So how does an extremely attractive woman[2] cope? By not becoming attached to the attention she receives, and reminding herself, "Beauty is a gift, but will I be saved?" so as to maintain a perspective on what is really important. She needs to let her Christianity prevail even if it means downplaying her attractiveness in social situations. I know this sounds like cultural heresy, but remember that God did not create feminine beauty so women could become vain and narcissistic. An emphasis on beauty tends to make a man crazy and the woman so desired that she may not develop a good personality or Christian humility, not to mention the other virtues. The attractive woman who tries to over-enhance her beauty is going to draw too much attention to herself. If she wants to attract a virtuous man, she should be restrained in her make-up, hair style, choice of jewelry and clothing styles. The goal for all women, regardless of their natural beauty, should be to look classy, not flashy.

The woman who has a soft, feminine beauty will find it far easier to find the right sort of Christian man than the one who tries to attract attention.

Remember that only interior beauty lasts forever. The following words from Scripture apply to all women:

> Let not yours be the outward adorning with braiding of
> hair, decoration of gold, and wearing of fine clothing, but let
> it be the hidden person of the heart with the imperishable

jewel of a gentle and quiet spirit, which in God's sight is very precious. (1 Peter 3: 3,4)

A bit of a cultural revolution is in order when it comes to women's dress. Granted, it's time for men to step up and take some sort of leadership role in the moral renewal of our culture but women have their part to play as well. Women have the most to gain from chastity, and modesty is a good way for them to begin.

Men Coping With Feminine Immodesty

There are two issues for men dealing with the dress of women. The first has to do with his own coping in the face of immodesty. The second has to do with how to bring up the topic of modest clothing in general.

So what does a man do to avoid being influenced negatively by an immodestly dressed woman? Some say look down, or look away, but this can be difficult. A better choice might be to look at her eyes, and in doing so, remind himself that she is a person, a child of God, not an object, and then look away. You might also say a short prayer that she might change her way of dressing, and realize better her dignity, as one created in the image of God.

If a woman shows up in something provocative on a first date you need to discover if she's a Catholic, or even a Christian. Then, you might discuss with her your ideas of courtship and bring up chastity, and modesty as part of that. Give her time to clue in. If she has no intention to get into the whole program of chastity and modesty, that's the time to say goodbye.

What if you've been going out for a while, she's a chastity-minded Christian, and she suddenly shows up in something provocative?

You might say something like, "You look gorgeous in that outfit, but it's making it hard for me to remain chaste when you're dressed that way." If she has any sense, she'll get the message and change. If she doesn't get it, you may have to come right out and say, "That outfit is too sexy for me. Can you please put on something a little less revealing?"

What if it's a Catholic friend, someone you're not dating, who shows up in a revealing outfit? Well, for the love of God, and her best interests, you could say, "Someone as pretty as you doesn't need to dress like that. You have so much more to offer than sex appeal."

If she is puzzled, you might continue, "Well, the way you're dressed, guys will be hard-pressed to focus on your personality." Prepare for a cold stare or even a slap in the face. Offer it to the Lord as a sacrifice for sins.

Is it worth the risk to speak up? Yes, if there is the slightest hope of improvement. Most Christian women are willing to change, even if their first reaction might be rather cool. Often it's simply a matter of getting people to think about this subject which is so foreign to our world. Consider the souls that might be saved, or at least the lives that might be improved by an increased awareness of modesty.

Summing It Up

Women need to realize that men are far more physical than women. They should consider their dress in the light of Christianity, and allow Christ and his mother, Mary to be their norm, not the world of fashion. They should try to help men think chastely, by selecting clothing that is fashionable, but not trendy; classy but not flashy.

Perhaps not everyone in the world is ready to hear about modesty, but many Catholics and other Christians are. Modesty is a virtue best taught by example, particularly the example of other women. It is rooted in prudence and the wisdom of selecting appropriate attire for each time and place. And it is based in love and charity. We can convince others of the values if we're patient and persevering. Once we convince them, they'll convince the world by their joy.

Endnotes

1.   This is a slightly expanded version of an article by the author, "A Modesty Proposal," published in *New Covenant* Magazine in August, 1999.

2.   This may not be such a politically correct topic in our "post-beauty" culture, but a priest must minister to everyone, especially those at risk for their salvation.

Chapter Seven

The Biblical Roles of Courtship[1]

A Biblical pattern for courtship not only exists, it is supported by some of our modern psychology. This pattern, which was well known in past eras, is making a comeback in the twenty-first century. What's so good about it is that it establishes a wonderful foundation for a healthy marriage.

Consider for starters the Old Testament story of Jacob and Rachel. Jacob worked seven years for Rachel's father, Laban, to win her in marriage. Somehow Laban tricked Jacob into marrying his older daughter Leah instead, and Jacob had to work another seven years to get Rachel. And look at David. He was offered the hand of Michal if he would slay a hundred Philistines. He came back with the evidence and claimed his bride. Can you imagine Rachel working seven or fourteen years to win the hand of Jacob? Or Michal doing some great deed to win David?

The woman of faith needs to realize she is a great "prize." In Proverbs 31:10 and following we read:

> When one finds a worthy wife,
> her value is far beyond pearls.

Her husband, entrusting his heart to her,
has an unfailing prize.
She brings him good, and not evil,
all the days of her life.
She reaches out her hands to the poor,
and extends her arms to the needy.
Her husband is prominent at the city gates
as he sits with the elders of the land.
She is clothed with strength and dignity,
and she laughs at the days to come.
She opens her mouth in wisdom,
and on her tongue is kindly counsel.
She watches the conduct of her household,
and eats not her food in idleness.
Her children rise up and praise her;
her husband, too, extols her:
"Many are the women of proven worth,
but you have excelled them all."
Charm is deceptive and beauty fleeting;
the woman who fears the LORD is to be praised.
Give her a reward of her labors,
and let her works praise her at the city gates. (NAB)

In Sirach we find, "Dismiss not a sensible wife; /a gracious wife is more precious than corals"; "A good wife is a generous gift, / bestowed on him who fears the LORD"; "A wife is her husband's richest treasure."[2] In Proverbs 12:4 we find, "A worthy wife is the crown of her husband" (NAB).

This is not to say that a good husband is not a prize too. But the Scriptures speak of the good wife — and not the good husband —

as a prize to emphasize their roles in marriage and courtship. The point is that the man is designed to pursue the woman, as an athlete pursues a victory, a victory which must be won over and over. This active pursuit by the man develops a healthy pattern which will carry over into the marriage and keep the marriage healthy. We see the same theme over and over in mythology: the hero goes out, slays the dragon, and wins the hand of his fair maiden. Psychologist Carl Jung, among others, was a great advocate of the importance of mythology for understanding the human soul.

What do the Scriptures have to say about husbands? Not that they are the prize, but that they should love their wives: "Husbands love your wives even as Christ loved the Church and handed himself over for her. . . . Husbands should love their wives as their own bodies . . ." (Ephesians 5:25, 28). "Husbands love your wives and avoid any bitterness toward them" (Colossians 3:19). Only in Titus 2:4 does Scripture speak of women loving their husbands, in an exhortation to the older women to "be reverent" so they can teach the younger women to "love their husbands and children."

Why do the Scriptures encourage only the husbands to love their wives? I would speculate that men are to be the initiators of love, of divine love (*agape*) in marriage. From my experience, it seems that wives who are loved by their husbands, in a truly self-giving way, have little trouble loving their husbands. So, the woman is the prize and the man is to pursue the prize by his love.

To an older generation this may seem obvious, but to the younger generation, it isn't. Girls start calling and pursuing boys in high school or younger nowadays and continue through college and beyond. This is not good news for women. Now, one might argue that the Scriptural evidence could be time-conditioned, and indeed, it could. But if there is confirmation in psychology, then the evidence stands.

Martians and Venusians

In the best seller, *Men Are from Mars, Women from Venus*, psychologist John Gray points out that men tend to value "power, competency, efficiency and achievement. They are always doing things to prove themselves and develop their power and skills." They are goal oriented. Women, says Gray, are into "love, communication, beauty and relationships . . ." and "helping and nurturing."

Also, when a man cares for a woman he often needs to retreat for a time before he becomes more intimate. A man needs to separate, to experience his individuality, his autonomy. He needs "some space." This, Gray says, is perfectly normal, and should not be cause for alarm. This is not time for the woman to take up the slack, he says. She needs to give the man room, and wait him out. Then, the man may bounce right back with gusto after a short time. Gray calls this the "rubber band theory."

If the man pursues the woman, and the woman allows herself to be pursued, this can work fine. He withdraws and she waits him out. However, if he is retreating and she decides that as a liberated woman, she should pursue him, he will run.

Gray's book certainly struck a chord in many: it was on the best seller list for several years. I think he gives ample evidence that a man's role is to pursue and a woman's to be pursued.

The Rules

Another book which confirms the "prize" theory is *The Rules* by Ellen Fein and Sherrie Schneider. This is not as tightly or soberly argued as *Men Are From Mars* but it makes some good points. These authors argue, sometimes whimsically, that women should let men do the chasing and women should insist that the men treat them right.

Here are a few of their "rules":

1. "Be a 'creature unlike any other.' . . . You don't settle. You don't chase anyone. You don't use sex to make men love you."[3] (In other words, you are the prize. This is especially true if you are a committed Christian.)
2. "Don't talk to a man first (and don't ask him to dance)."
3. "Don't meet him halfway or go Dutch on a date." Whoever asks a person out for a date should pay for it. So, if you let him ask, you can let him pay. If you make it too easy for him he may well lose interest.
4. "Don't accept a Saturday night date after Wednesday." Make plans for the weekend every Thursday morning, whether it be to wash your hair or visit family and stick to it. Be polite, but firm.
5. "Let him take the lead."

These are some of their better "rules." Unfortunately, coming from a secular perspective, they don't uphold one of the best "rules" for a healthy courtship — "no sex, period."

Although they overstate their case at times, their fundamental thesis is accurate, namely that women should allow men to pursue them, and women should insist on good treatment. By developing a pattern of respect in the courtship, women are not just using a trick to get a man, but laying the foundation for a lifelong healthy relationship in marriage. The authors point out that their grandmothers knew all this very well. Alas, the modern woman doesn't; she's been sold a bill of goods.

Some people think *The Rules* are manipulative. If they are used for manipulation, i.e., getting a man to do what he doesn't want to do, forget it. In that case you'd be establishing the foundation for a miserable marriage. But if they are used to simply help the man prize his woman, as most good men really want to, then they are worthwhile.

Remember too, the rules are not about *playing* hard to get. They are about *being* hard to get. If you're a good religious woman with your act together, you don't have to settle for ragged treatment. You're a prize, so you should act like one.

Some have claimed that these conventional roles make women subject to men, submissive partners, going along with men's designs. This is not what many women are finding in practice. Paradoxically, the woman who lets the man pursue her and plan the date (this isn't power; it's *hard work!*) has far more equality than the woman who does the pursuing. As Christians, we believe in the equality of personal dignity, not the equality of interchangeability so often touted today. It is precisely through these "old-fashioned" gender roles that the natures of both the man and woman are fulfilled and mutual respect is upheld.

Winnefred Cutler in *Searching for Courtship* points out that when women ask men out, "the men often love it, may even accept the date, but courtship does not follow. And, in most cases, neither does marriage." She quotes a young woman, a graduate of Bryn Mawr College, who believed that it made no difference who asked, the man or the woman. When she courted a man and developed a great relationship, she thought all was fine. But, then he proposed to someone else. She was crushed. She wrote, "Women taking the kind of lead I did learn . . . one way or the other . . . although we were told we had the right, it doesn't work."

Sex-Free Courtship Fosters Respect

Saying no to premarital sex is another plus for the woman. I mentioned in Chapter Four the woman who realized she was a slave if she had sex with her man, and the one who felt free enough to break up with her man when she stopped sleeping with him. Another woman stopped sleeping with her boyfriend and he still didn't treat her right. She kept pulling back to the point of starting to date other men. She refused to put up with his poor treatment of her. Finally, he woke up (a few do) and started to treat her like a queen. Both benefited. She got a civilized husband and he got a wife he could respect.

Some women are afraid to insist that their man treat them right, or to refuse to sleep with him, for fear of losing him. In fact, a woman has nothing to lose. If she stands firm, either the man will straighten out and treat her with respect, or he will refuse to treat her right and leave. Either way she wins. If she gives in and takes the trash behavior she loses both ways. Either she keeps a man who will treat her badly for life, or he ends up having so little respect for her that she loses him anyway.

The man who disrespects or denigrates his wife ruins things for both himself and his wife. She may come to have little self-respect and confidence. He, then, will be turned off by his mouse of a wife, whom he helped to create, and be miserable himself. Happy the man who treats his wife like a queen. His wife will make him feel like a king.

Are there exceptions to this dichotomy? Sure, both men and women have to insist on respect, and some men settle for too little respect, but this is rare. Generally, if a woman likes a man she treats him with respect. However, vice versa is not always the case.

Bishop Fulton J. Sheen said with great insight that the level of civilization of any society is always determined by the women. If women refuse to give in to premarital sex, and insist that men treat them well before and during marriage, they will raise up the level of the whole culture.

I am convinced, from my observations of single adults, that a key purpose of courtship is for men to learn to be civilized and respectful, and to learn the value of affection without sex, and for women to learn to discipline their love. Men need to discover the art of loving in a spiritual and affective, but non-sexual way. Women need to moderate their emotions by reason, and stay cool enough to let the man pursue them, until he commits. The women who behave this way are far more successful in love than the "liberated" ones who do not.

Respect and Self-confidence

Although chastity is key here, and goes far to help maintain the woman's proper place in marriage and the family, there's more to it than that. It's also about dignity and respect. Granted, the decline of respect for women is rooted in the sexual revolution, but alas, we all breathe the air of this sad phenomenon. Everyone, even those who live chastely, have to deal with the problem of disrespect.

How does a woman insist on respect without becoming a nag? In a nutshell, when a man treats her disrespectfully, she doesn't lose her temper. She just withdraws a bit, and says something like, "We need to talk." When they do talk, she tells him in a quiet time why she is unhappy. If he doesn't shape up after several warnings, she needs to tell him, "This is not working so well. I think we should go out with other people." And, of course, she must be ready to follow through on that. If he doesn't change, it's time to forget him.

Along this same line, self-confidence is extremely important in women. Every man should say every honest thing possible to help build the self-confidence of a young woman. Not arrogance, not pride, not manipulative powers, but self-confidence. Every devout Christian woman should have a genuine, while humble, awareness of her great value — that she is a great prize.

Summing It Up

The Bible gives an indication as to the roles of men and women in courtship: the man is the pursuer and the woman is the prize. This is confirmed by modern psychology and experience. By not having premarital sex, a woman will receive more respect from her husband, respect which could last a lifetime. Even without sex, she must still insist on respectful treatment if she wishes to have a good marriage. By insisting on chastity and proper treatment, she has nothing to lose, but a bad boyfriend or worse, a disastrous marriage.

Women have taken the brunt of the sexual revolution. It's time for them to reclaim their dignity and self-respect, not only with regard to chastity, but with regard to the whole of courtship and marriage. Once they do, both men and women will benefit.

Endnotes

1. This chapter is adapted from an article by the author published in *Laywitness* in July 2000, entitled "Women: The Key to Cultural Renewal."

2. Sir. 7:19; 26:3; 36:24, *New American Bible*.

3. Ellie Fein and Sherrie Schneider, *The Rules*, New York: Warner Books, 1995, pp. 22, 23.

Chapter Eight

Christian Courtship Strategies

Have you ever considered where American dating patterns developed? Hollywood and television. Considering the marital success rates of the people in these industries, I don't think we should take our cue from them.

Today, there is far too much pressure on young men and women when they go out. It's too "clingy." They are, in effect, expected to commit to dating each other exclusively from the second or third date. Far better to get together as friends for various activities for a time, without the pressure that exclusive dating usually brings. This means you see each other and do things together, but you are free to go out with others[1] if you wish. There's no kissing goodnight, or even holding hands. Nice, warm, chaste hugs are fine, since good friends often hug, but everything is low key and low pressure. There's no "I love you" just "You're a great friend," or "You are so sweet!" Getting together once a week and talking on the phone twice a week is the level of commitment.

If the friendship grows deeper you can move into a more exclusive arrangement. Agree to not date others, get together twice a week and speak on the phone a bit more. But until you both agree to move into courtship, keep it just a friendship, even if an exclusive one.

What if one or the other starts to have strong romantic feelings? That's fine, but until you agree on a courtship, don't let them take over and govern your behavior. Don't express those strong feelings in words, just in kindness and consideration.

One woman agreed to a friendship scenario and while they were speaking one evening, the question of exclusiveness came up. Her friend told her he was seeing another woman as well. She became quite upset and told him she couldn't accept that, because she had strong feelings for him. So they stopped going out. She asked me what I thought.

I told her I believed he would have been better not mentioning that he was seeing someone else. Nonetheless, his going out with someone else was not wrong, since they hadn't agreed on an exclusive relationship. Additionally, I thought she would have been better telling him she needed to think about it, without ending the relationship on the spot. Had she told him "I guess I was presuming too much," and continued to go out with him, a real courtship (which is, by definition, exclusive) might have followed.

The idea of friendship dating once a week having to be exclusive is, in my opinion, a holdover from the clingy trial-marriage style of dating that has produced a 50 percent divorce rate. If you insist on exclusiveness for early friendship dating, you are going to slide back into the old pattern.

Sometimes the woman has to tell the man what she wants in terms of friendship dating. One woman simply told her date, "I'd like to move slowly here and just date as friends without kissing for a couple of months. I hope you're okay with that." He was. They had a great time for that period and later he actually thanked her for insisting on that approach.

Had he not been open to her idea, she would probably have said, "Please think about it. It's important to me." If he wants to shorten the time, that should be negotiable, but if he wants no part of that approach, she might ask what he does want and decide from that if she wants to pursue this relationship.

One of the benefits of a "friendship first" approach is that it provides something quite positive for couples to aim at before the courtship begins. When I was young, we used to think in terms of getting through the first three dates, so we could have a goodnight kiss. As time went on, it got reduced to two dates, and then there was no waiting. A goodnight kiss was expected on the first date. This was all rather utilitarian, rather calculated. And, it was really not very personal. Friendship dating is not biding time until the first kiss and the implied commitment to exclusiveness on the third or fourth date. It's a wonderful, gentle way to lay a good foundation for a chaste courtship.

One of the key elements of a Christian life is living by reason. More and more young men and women are examining their own dating behavior and realizing that some major changes are needed. "Would not my spiritual life be better and my life as a medical student be simpler if I just developed some good friendships for a while, and didn't rush into an intense relationship, when I'm a few years away from being able to marry?" It is a delight, although admittedly a limited one, to have a good, strong friendship with a person of the opposite sex. It is a joy to have someone you can discuss your life with and feel confident you won't be exploited by that person. It is sweet to be able to chastely hug a person you really like and trust. More and more young people are seeing the value of slowing down, and "smelling the roses" in the garden of friendship.

How do you move from friendship dating to courtship? The man says to the woman, "Well, we've seen each other for two months as friends. Would you be open to a courtship now?" If she asks what he means by that, he says, "Would you allow me to pursue this relationship with a view to possible marriage if things work out?" She might say, "That would be nice," or, if she's not ready for that, she might say, "Could we continue on for another month and then decide." (There's always the possibility she might say, "No, I'm not interested in that." If it's the latter, the man can let her go and move on himself.)

If she doesn't know what she wants after three months, she should tell him she doesn't want to get into a courtship with him. If he is willing to continue to date as friends to see if anything develops, and she is willing, fine. Or, they could cool things down a bit and continue to get together from time to time and talk on the phone. Sometimes women take a long time, even years, to decide they love a man. A man has to take into consideration things like his age, her age, his own readiness for marriage, and so forth when a woman says she needs more than three months. This is something he should take into prayer, seeking the Lord's guidance.

What if *she* is ready to move into a courtship and he doesn't make a move? If the man is to take the lead, as we suggested earlier, then let him lead. He should be the one to propose moving from casual friendship dating to an exclusive friendship, or courtship after one or two or three months. However, if after three months she thinks he is taking too much time, and she wants to move on if he is not going to commit to a courtship, she can speak up. She might just ask him, "Do you see our relationship as leading to something more than a friendship?" The problem with that is, he may say no (although most women have a good idea of what he is intending). Despite the danger of that, I think it's the best approach. If she feels hesitant, she might try a more subtle approach, such as the following story illustrates.

A young woman once told me she had been going out with a man for three months, but she wasn't sure what his intentions were. She asked if I thought she should tell him how much she cared for him so as to get things going. I told her "No way. He should start that kind of talk."

"Well then, Father, what should I do? We've been going out for three months and he's never even kissed me."

"Next time you go out, when he takes you home, back up against the door jam and say, 'You may kiss me if you like.' "

About a year later I heard they were getting married. I guess it worked.

What if a man is not interested in a courtship after three months? Forget him. Men usually know long before three months.

What if the woman asks if he sees the relationship leading to something more, and he says yes, but doesn't move into courtship soon thereafter? Then she should say, "I'm not sure we should go out any more." If he asks why, she should say, "Well, I don't think you're ready for courtship." If he says that he is trying to move slowly, she can simply say directly, "I'm not happy with continuing at this level."

This may seem a bit assertive for the Christian woman, but enough is enough. By saying up front she is willing to end the relationship, she is not manipulating him. If he was intending to become more serious, now is the time. If not, it's time for both to move on.

Regardless of your situation, I strongly recommend trying to simply develop a low-key friendship with someone, without any kissing or romance for one to three months before getting into a more romantic sort of courtship. A number of people are opting for this sort of relationship for a time, to see if they are compatible as friends, and then, if all goes well, beginning a courtship. Others begin such a relationship with no clue that it might lead to a courtship, and much to their surprise it does! Some of the best marriages have begun with a beautiful friendship.

Are You Ready for Courtship?

One of the things that is getting more attention nowadays is the phenomenon of younger people dating seriously without the slightest prospect of being able to get married. Often this comes up with teenagers, but it can apply to young adults as well. Joshua Harris' book *I Kissed Dating Goodbye* sold thousands and thousands of copies, because he made some good points, including, "if two people can't make a commitment to each other, they don't have any business pursuing romance."

Connie Marshner wrote an article[2] some time back in which she pointed out that the dating habits of our teenagers are a perfect preparation for divorce, not marriage. When young people pair off and pursue an intimate relationship with no real likelihood of marriage, they are asking for trouble. First, there is the problem of temptations against chastity. There is a desire to bond with this person, to get close to them, and alas, is so often the case even with adult dating patterns, draw all the pleasure possible from the relationship. Even if the two didn't want to get into sexual relations, they feel compelled to by their emotions and their closeness. Another problem is the emotional roller-coaster they go through. Marshner calls it "repeated intimacy and heartbreak." This, she says, is a "pattern which paves the way for every divorce."

Granted, both Harris and Marshner are speaking of younger people, but something similar can happen when young adults play at courtship when they are really not ready for marriage. Take, for example, the man — or woman — who is just starting law school or medical school. Or, the person who knows he/she doesn't want to get married for at least five or six years. Should they be intensely dating, as if they were in a position to get married?

I would suggest that those who are in such a situation think about it and see if their life might not be a lot more pleasant if they were just to see members of the opposite sex casually, as friends, preferably in groups, not as lovers. Otherwise emotions may get carried away, and bring the physical side of things along with it.

Granted, emotions can get stirred up with a strong friendship dating relationship too, but there is a difference. In the friendship scenario, if you don't express those feelings verbally and you don't kiss, you're not fanning the emotional flame. In this way, you have a better chance of keeping things under control. It's not that in this sort of friendship situation a person can't enjoy these feelings. But, for the sake of a healthy courtship at the right time, he or she simply enjoys the friendship, which is a beautiful thing in itself, rather than expressing a desire to commit, which is not realistic at the time.

Now some people may be thinking, "Father, I'm thirty-five years old. I can't spend three months just as friends. We need to get on with this." Many a poor soul has lived to regret such an attitude. Others will say, "But my Aunt Maggie had a whirlwind courtship — six months — and she has a great marriage." I'm sure she does, but for every Aunt Maggie there are ten or twenty Aunt Imogenes who have had terrible marriages because they rushed things.

Rushing things in courtship is one of the most common reasons for bad marriages and divorce. In the mid-eighties researchers at Kansas State University studied marital satisfaction in relation to time of courtship. The results? "Couples who had dated for more than two years scored consistently high on marital satisfaction, while couples who had dated for shorter periods scored in a wide range from very high to very low."[3] Based on that, and on what I've seen, I would recommend at least a two year courtship before marriage. For some people, who are daily communicants, well-versed in the saints, and who are over 30, eighteen months might be acceptable, but no less.

People come up with all sorts of excuses to shorten the courtship. They want time to have a certain number of children. Grandma will be here for a visit and we want her to see our wedding. We're older. We know what we want. Remember, love is the form of marriage. Everything flows from that. If you don't get that right because you rushed things and made a wrong choice, you'll be defeating your purpose. And, you'll be miserable. Is that what you want to risk?

Many women over thirty tend to be in a big hurry to get married. One of our women, a bright, charming devout Catholic, was thirty-eight when a young man swept her off her feet. He seemed to be a good Catholic, and a good man overall. They met in February and by September they were married. By the following September he was filing for divorce.

Another thing not to focus on is the biological clock! One woman got married at age forty and proceeded to have three children. It's not the easiest way to do things, but God has a plan for

you, and if you do things according to his plan, he'll bring it to
fruition. No woman should ever accept a proposal of marriage before she has been seeing a man for at least a year. If they qualify for
the 30-plus, daily communicant exemption, they might have a short
engagement, six or seven months. That gives them a year and a
half to get to know each other. That, with lots of prayer, and some
rational thinking should be enough for two devout people over
thirty. Think about it. If you get married, you'll be together for
perhaps forty, fifty, even sixty years. What's another six or eight
months?

One couple came to me in April to arrange a September wedding. They had only been dating a few months, so I didn't feel right
about it. I asked her what the hurry was, and she said, "Well, I've
had bad luck with long courtships." What she meant was that she
had wasted about five years on a guy who never committed and she
didn't want to do the same thing again. Also, she was thirty-three
years old. She was clock-watching.

I told them both, "I'm really very uncomfortable with a September time frame for this wedding. I would urge you to wait at
least a couple of months. Please go and pray about this and come
back to me." (Whenever a priest says "pray about it," that means
he disagrees with your plan.)

They did pray about it and they agreed to wait until November.
We went through all the preparations and everything was in order.
In September she came to me to tell me that the wedding was off
because she had decided he wasn't the one for her. They avoided a
real disaster by waiting.

Now, some might ask about the sexual temptations in a long
courtship. The solution is the real virtue of chastity, not cutting
short the courtship which will only diminish your chances of suc-

cess in the marriage. Real chastity is not like holding your breath until you find a licit outlet. It's a virtue you need to develop for life. It's living in peace with your sexual appetite, whether married or not. It's not a short-term fix, but a part of real Christian living.

If you convert your heart to believe that chastity is the way to happiness, and commit to gentle good night kisses, tender affection and lots of chaste hugs, a long courtship should not be a major problem. You will be growing in spiritual intimacy which will bring real joy. This approach really works. It establishes a foundation of focusing on the person rather than the body, a great foundation for courtship and marriage.

Some may argue, "Well, you can't make any rules on courtship length. Since people are so different, you have to look at things case by case." Good try, but what are the criteria? Maturity? How do you measure that? Religious conviction? That takes time to evaluate in a sweetheart. Adaptability? Generosity? Many people have proven they can be generous and adaptable for several months, but not for two years. There are so many dysfunctional people today, it's harder than ever to discern a person's character. The only hope you have is to pray hard, use your head, and play the percentages by giving the relationship enough time to develop. Then, if the marriage is a disaster, you can at least say before God, "I did my part!" Think in terms of at least two years from the day you began to see each other once or twice a week, until marriage. You won't regret it.

Remember: *Short courtships often make for short marriages.*

Avoid Over-dating

One of the things that goes with the Western gorging mentality is to over-date, that is, to date too many times a week. We all have jobs, friends, our prayer life, family, recreation, and those things take time. When we start courting it just doesn't make sense to drop half your life so you can be with a person five or six nights a week. You've got to maintain your own life. Sometimes when some of our women or men fall in love, we hardly ever see them anymore. This could be the beginning of a co-dependent relationship. Or, it could be a sign that one or both think that this person is going to "fulfill all my dreams." They may protest, "Oh no. I realize no person on earth can ever fulfill me completely," but subconsciously that is exactly what they are indicating by this behavior. One couple came to me for pre-marital counseling and the woman said she wasn't sure her fiancé was the right man for her because he was always tired. He seemed unable to cope with life. When it was his turn, he told me he was tired a lot because he saw his fiancée about six nights a week. And, he lived half an hour away! When the three of us met together I told her it was no wonder the poor man was tired. They were seeing each other too much. Two or three times a week should be enough.

She said, "Well, when we see each other a lot we feel good about each other."

I told her, "It's not a matter of feelings. It's about what is smart and prudent. It just doesn't make sense to see each other that much. Courtship is stressful. It should be done in moderation."

Some couples discover a certain staleness when they see each other too often. The cure is to stop seeing each other so much. There is such a thing as creative absence. Give yourselves two or three days a week when you don't even call. You'll find a certain zip the next day.

Now of course, it's a little tricky backing off when you've been overdoing things. You can't simply say, "I think we should see each other less often." This could bring on real problems. Perhaps the man might say something like, "I feel like I'm not providing as much for you as I would like in this relationship. I want us to have more fun when we are together. I think I'm smothering you. Let's try an experiment next week. I'll call you Monday and Wednesday and Friday and let's play tennis Saturday, followed by a nice quiet dinner. Then on Sunday, let's go to a late Mass and then have a picnic in the park. Then on Monday you can let me know how you are feeling. Sound good?" Notice he puts the blame on himself, and offers her something in return for her consent, more fun and things to look forward to.

Women have told me in the past, "Father, he's always there. I need a night here and there to wash my hair and just relax. I need a day when I can do my laundry and get all my errands done. I can't do that with him around. It's not polite." So, if she's the one wanting a little more space, she could say something similar. "Sweetheart, I think we're wearing out our welcome. Let's just get together two or three times this week and see if that works out better." Then if he tries to plan too many things, she gently reminds him of their little experiment, "Remember we were going to try a slightly different schedule this week?" and go from there.

My own sister had this problem of over-dating. She was seeing her fiancé so often that she could hardly wake up for work each morning. She was tired all the time. Finally, my parents convinced her to slow down and limit the number of dates each week. It worked.

One night during the week (and this should be optional) and a couple of nights on the weekend (or one night and one daytime weekend date) should be enough. Certainly a phone call every other day or so as well wouldn't hurt. Of course, there will be some weekends when a couple will go to visit their families, or go on a chaperoned camping or ski trip. But if there is this intense need to see the other person every day, the marriage could end up as a real co-dependency. There could be a real inability to function without having a "fix" from your sweetheart.

Worse yet, you could end up with an *egoisme à deux*, as the French put it. You try to draw every ounce of pleasure from this person while closing out every one and every thing that could interfere with that pleasure, including children in marriage. Of course, when the emotional love diminishes, as it always does, then there's a huge let-down. It's a sure path to misery. Balance is the key to a happy courtship, and a happy life.

Can't Get No Satisfaction?

Sometimes people date merely to have pleasure and enjoy themselves. Now of course, courtship should be pleasant. You shouldn't keep courting someone who consistently makes you miserable. But, courtship is not about having a peak experience on every date. It's about discovering if you are compatible with someone, about seeing if this person can exercise self-giving love (*agape*) and showing this person you can exercise that same love. It's also about exploring a friendship and building friendship. It should be pleasant, but having one or two disappointing dates among many good ones, does not mean you're not compatible.

If you're just looking for "satisfaction" on a date, think again. Dating is really about relating in a truly Christian way, not as high-schoolers, trying to draw all the pleasure you can from this person, but as godly adults, trying to see if you might have a vocation to become life-long partners. This involves not just receiving, but giving as well.

The attitude should not be "How am I going to enjoy myself tonight?" but "How can I serve this person in love so as to build a good relationship? How can I get to know this person? What can I do to make her/him happy?" If you approach a date that way, you may find that you will enjoy yourself, and even more important, your date will enjoy herself/himself.

Remnants of Hedonism

A young woman came to see me once while she was on vacation from her studies in England. Her boyfriend was coming over to visit and to do some sight-seeing with her and she wanted to know if it would be okay for him to stay with her and her roommate while he was there. I told her no way. It could give scandal, and a woman should never, under ordinary circumstances, allow a man the intimacy of spending the night in her living quarters. It tends to destroy her mystique, which she should maintain until her wedding day. Remember, ladies, you're the ones who must restore the culture. It has always been primarily the women who have upheld civilization in our world.

To be sure, there are some qualifications here. Is it appropriate for a woman to invite her man to come with her to visit her family in another state, and for them to provide him a room, apart from hers? Certainly, especially if the normal Christian precautions are taken. (It helps if the rooms aren't adjoining.)

Is it appropriate for a woman to go off on a pilgrimage or tour to Europe or the Holy Land with her boyfriend with several others, each staying in a different room? No problem. Certainly a couple wishing to violate that situation could do so as well, but the setup is reasonable for devout Christians, especially since the usual arrangement is for each to have a roommate of the same sex.

But some of the things that people of faith do are simply mind-boggling. One couple living chastely — the woman was a daily communicant — went on vacation together for a few days, sharing the same room. I asked the woman, who had been coming to me for spiritual direction, "You didn't ask your spiritual director, huh?" She assured me that nothing happened but when I asked if they had a good time, she said it was awful.

"Well, good," I replied. "That's a blessing. Think about this for a minute. You come and go from the same room every day. Do the people staying there know you're not having sex? You can't very well put a sign on the door saying 'for those who might care, we want you to know that we are not having sex in here.' And what if someone staying there sees you in church, receiving Communion. Are they going to think the Church has changed its teaching on chastity? Or will they think, 'Here's another hypocritical Catholic who receives the Eucharist sacrilegiously?' And, this is to say nothing of the temptations involved in such a situation. Can you imagine Mary, if she were living today, staying with Joseph for a few days during their courtship?"

These are what I call the "remnants of hedonism." People really want to live the faith, but they have some left over blind spots with regard to decency. Being a Christian means not only living the faith, but also avoiding giving the appearance of wrong-doing to others. Some say, "If you get the wrong idea, it's because you have a dirty mind."

Not so. If someone presumes that you are doing what 98 percent of other people are doing in the same situation, it's not their fault, it's yours. The Scriptures make it clear that we are responsible for the scandal we give others. As Jesus put it, ". . . it would be better for anyone who leads astray one of these little ones who believe in me, to be drowned by a millstone around his neck in the depths of the sea . . . woe to the one through whom scandal comes!" (Matthew 18:6, 7). In Matthew 17:27 Jesus shows Peter that they are exempt from the temple tax, but then adds that Peter should pay the tax, "for fear of disedifying them." All that we do that even gives the appearance of wrong-doing can have a bad influence on others, and we are responsible for that influence.

Another couple I knew was about to get married. I had to talk to the bride-to-be about something and when I called her number I got the phone company's recording, "This number has been changed to the following number. . . ." It was the fiancé's number! Now, this woman was a daily communicant, a devout Catholic. They had been doing everything right. I was broken-hearted.

So, I called them. The fiancé answered and told me that they were living together but had separate bedrooms. When I pointed out that people would be scandalized, she moved into a hotel. They confessed that they hadn't thought about the scandal it would give to others. Her lease had run out, and, "it seemed like a good way to save money."

One of the things a good Christian does is to think, and to try to do so with the mind of Christ. The little bracelets and pins which read "WWJD" (What would Jesus do?) are not proposing some sweet little sentiment but a commitment to a radically different way of life different from our pagan world.

I was speaking to a single woman and a young married man some time ago at a friend's wedding. The young woman told me unabashedly that the two of them had lived together (they weren't dating) with two other people in a "coed house." I responded in my usual blustery way, "Shame on you."

She said, "No, Father, we were just friends. Nothing went on there."

"I didn't think you guys were having sex. Shame on you anyway." I went into my mantra about putting a notice on the door to tell every neighbor that nothing illicit was going on inside.

He smiled and said, "I think I kind of knew that, Father." Somewhere he had vaguely picked up the fact that a good Christian not only tries to live chastely, but also tries to cultivate an environment which makes it easier for *everyone* to live chastely.

Finally, here is the testimony of a young couple who moved in together chastely and came to realize how wrong it was:

> We did not see anything wrong with buying and sharing a house, provided that we left out the sex . . . we bought a house together and shared a bed for a year before our wedding, and we saved sexual intercourse until we were married.
>
> However, after several years of marriage and spiritual growth (fueled in part by using [natural family planning] . . .) we realized that what we did was wrong. Even without the sex, living together was wrong . . .
>
> We deeply regret that our families, our friends (even close ones), and our neighbors — who all knew we are Roman Catholics — assumed we were fornicating . . .
>
> We brought shame on our Church. Our examples as the oldest children in our families may have contributed to the choices of some younger siblings to cohabitate. One or two friends may have gotten the wrong idea, too. Someday we will have to explain to our son (now turning three) that we are not examples to follow in this matter. The term that describes all these ill effects is "scandal" which is leading

others to temptation and sin, and bringing shame upon a
religion or community.

. . . Even though we waited for intercourse, we shared
moments at a level of intimacy that God probably intended
for marital bonding, moments like arousing caresses and
kisses, falling asleep in each other's arms, waking up together.
. . . It is the familial daily sharing of these that is God's gift to
cement a marriage. We should have waited. . . . [4]

Is giving scandal so bad? Well, let's put it this way. Suppose your
bad example was the deciding factor in another couple's decision
to live together (unchastely). Is that bad enough?

One last thought on this subject. Your boyfriend lives an hour
away. It's late and he's tired. What should you do? Presuming there's
not a blizzard or a real crisis, give him some strong coffee and send
him home. There is simply no way, short of an emergency, that a
woman should compromise her own mystique and give scandal by
letting a man stay overnight in her apartment. Nor should a Christian man ask.

Moving in Psychologically

Most good Christian couples would not dream of physically moving in with each other before marriage. But psychologically is another question.

What do we mean by moving in psychologically? For starters,
buying a house together. You may figure, "Well, we're going to get
married in a few months anyway. Let's buy a house together."

Here's the problem: you're not married. You're engaged. Being
engaged means you will spend time together to test your relation-

ship, to learn how to be faithful to just one person, to work on developing the habit of mutual respect. It doesn't mean you are committed. You are planning to get married, but you are not married. Marriage is the commitment, not the engagement. If you buy a house together, or a car, or whatever, you are implicitly saying, "We are committed." You are in some small way trivializing the wedding.

What if things don't work out? You not only have to break up, which is traumatic enough in itself, but you have to undo your financial merger. Some may even feel more pressure to marry because of their financial partnership. The only thing drawing you into a marriage with your fiancé should be the firm belief that this person is right for you, and vice versa, and that you can help each other get to the Kingdom. Mutually owned houses or cars or whatever should have nothing to do with it. Wait till you get married and then get into real estate.

Another thing that confuses things in the courtship is the giving of expensive gifts. This can be a manipulative thing. A woman may think, "I've got to marry him now, after all the things he's given me." And, he may think, "I have to marry her, now that I've made such an investment in her." Of course, with women now sometimes earning more than men, the reverse can be true as well. Expensive gifts can sometimes be a substitute for the essential gift in a relationship, the gift of self, the gift of one's time, one's interest, one's kindness, etc.

Another way of "psychologically moving in" is to leave lots of your belongings at his/her place. Don't do it! It's another extraneous bond that makes breaking up harder and weakens the significance of the wedding.

One more way of committing too soon is deciding this one's "right" after just a few months. This places a person, especially the woman, in a precarious situation. What if you decide he's "right" and he proposes after just six months? I have been through the it's "right" scenario twice. The women in each case were committed Catholics, from great families. Everything seemed so right, especially compared to other relationships that seemed so wrong. I had the rug pulled out from under me both times. It was very painful. So, for your own protection, guard your heart for at least the first year. Say, if you wish, "Everything seems right so far . . ." But don't fall into the trap of saying "He's the one," until you've been seeing each other at least a year. And even then, hold a little bit in reserve. Remember, you're not married until you're married. Every moment leading up to that is a time to test the relationship. You may change your mind at any moment before the wedding. Granted, the closer the wedding comes, the greater would have to be the conflict to call everything off, but if this person does something bizarre, you could call things off the night before, or even the day of, the wedding.

Don't commit until you commit. And then really commit!

Best Age for Marriage?

On the average, the ideal age for a couple to marry is late twenties. If both partners are devout, that is, daily Mass-goers, praying the Rosary or equivalent each day and reading the lives of the saints,[5] mid-twenties might be reasonable. This presumes, of course, that they are both mature and he has a good job and can support a family

Those marrying at 21 or 22 have double the divorce rate of those marrying at 24 or 25.[6] One study showed that those who married at age 28 had the most stable marriages.[7] Sociologists Marcia and Tom

Lasswell found that "divorce rates are lowest for those who marry for the first time at age 28 or later. The chances for a stable marriage increase as both partners reach the age of thirty, and then the rates level off."[8]

So do you just refuse to schedule your wedding until your twenty-eighth birthday? No, of course not. Just think about that as an ideal age in general, and avoid getting antsy about getting married earlier. For a woman, try to wait at least until you are 24 to get married, for a man, 26.[9] This way you double your chances of success. If you pass 26, and you have your head on straight, think in terms of "Any time now, Lord," and be very open to the possibility of meeting someone, having a nice leisurely courtship and, if all seems right, marrying. Getting to 28 doesn't guarantee anything, and you still have to work hard to discern if this is the right one, but it's just one more thing in your favor.

Again, smart people don't assume that they are a special case. Most of those who make major mistakes because of lack of age or length of courtship were convinced they were the exception.

Waiting too long can create problems as well, although I have met very few good Catholics who simply waited too long. Most of the time they haven't met the right person yet and are hurt when someone presumes they have just delayed marriage for selfish reasons. Nonetheless, marrying over thirty does have some special problems. It can be very difficult to adapt if you've been living the single life for ten or fifteen years after college, especially if you have lived alone. However, I have officiated at many weddings where one or both were 33 or over. Often, they needed counseling within a few months of the wedding. However, the good news is that when they went through counseling and really worked at improving, they were able to do quite well together, and find real happiness. These were dedicated Catholics who were highly motivated to have a life-long marriage. With that sort of commitment and a willingness to get counseling if needed, couples who marry in their mid-thirties can do very well.

Get a Job!

Another thing: a man should not propose to a woman until he has a good, solid job. This is not materialism, it's just plain decency. It's irresponsible for a man to ask a woman to marry him if he does not have the means to support her. I am amazed at the number of men who think nothing of asking a woman to marry them, when they do not have a good job. They are living in a dream world. I don't think a real man, a thinking man, a man of character would do that.

Been There, Done That

Some years back a divorced woman with an annulment came to see me. She wanted to know if there was any reason why she should not sleep with the man she was dating. After all, she was beyond her child-bearing years, so that wasn't an issue.

I told her the rules were the same for her as for any single woman. Sex belongs only in marriage, not only because it may produce children, but also because it is a sacred symbol of the marriage covenant. She accepted this, and resolved to live by it.

This is an issue which comes up surprisingly often among the widowed and divorced, especially those beyond menopause. Sometimes a man will say to a widowed or divorced woman, "Are you interested in living together?" as if because she has been married and has had children, things are somehow different with regard to morality. They aren't.

Both men and women in this situation need to make it clear to anyone they might date that they are committed to their faith, and chastity is part of that. Certainly this should be done graciously and gently, but firmly.

One of the difficulties faced in these situations is the tremendous sense of loss after the death of a spouse or a divorce. A person can be extremely vulnerable emotionally at this time, and look for someone to fill the void. Also, after divorce and annulment, one can feel a great loss of self-confidence. But finding a new partner right away is generally not the best solution to these problems.

There is no way around the sorrow that comes after losing a spouse. I watched my own mother struggle after my father died when she was just 60. That first year was, I am sure, the hardest year of her life. But, by her strong faith, and the support of her children and friends, she made it through, and built up her life again. Rebuilding your life is such an important thing after the loss of a spouse, far more important than finding a new partner right away. Once you "have a life" again, which can take a year or two or even longer, then you will have enough balance to approach courtship in a less vulnerable, more objective way.

The last thing you want to do as a Christian is give in to invitations for extramarital sex or worse yet, marry a divorced person without an annulment outside the Church, hoping to fill the void left by a former spouse. Immoral relationships don't heal the pain of losing a spouse, they just postpone it, and in the long run, increase it. It's only in a strong spiritual life through prayer, the sacraments, Mass, good works for others and in family and friends that real healing can be found. Once you have found healing, then you can, if you wish, pursue a new relationship, taking the time to develop a friendship first, and insisting on doing everything God's way. It's the only way to true happiness.

Annulments

Second marriages after divorce brings to mind the issue of annulments. By no means should a person date others if he or she is divorced but does not have an annulment. This would be a trivialization of marriage. Until you have an annulment in hand you should presume that you are still married in the eyes of God. It's true that most, as many as 90 percent of annulment applications are granted, but sometimes they are not. What happens to a couple who have proceeded to enter a courtship and then found that one or the other could not get an annulment? I urge you not to date until you actually have an annulment, and not to date anyone else who is divorced and does not have one. In fact, sometimes people refrain from getting an annulment so that they can have an excuse not to marry.

Many people find the annulment process bewildering. I often get questions such as, "I tried faithfully to live out my marriage, but my spouse left me for someone else. What can I do? How do I go about getting an annulment?"

To apply for an annulment, you must already be divorced by the civil court. Then you may proceed to contact your parish priest for an application.

If the previous marriage involving at least one Catholic was *not* in the Catholic Church there is a very brief annulment process. Simply go to the rectory and pick up the application for annulment due to "Lack of Form." If the previous marriage *was* recognized by the Church, you may seek an annulment by a "formal process." This involves getting a three-page application from the rectory and writing the story of your marriage which is then submitted to the marriage tribunal. This process takes about a year, although in some dioceses it may be longer or shorter. Some cost is involved, but marriage tribunals are usually most flexible about payment arrangements and many offer a sliding scale. In any event, you are not "paying" for your annulment, but helping to offset the administrative costs. Money should never be a reason for not applying for an annulment. Ask your parish priest about it when you first discuss the matter if it is a concern. As a Catholic, you have the right to pursue an annulment, regardless of your financial status.

Does an annulment affect legitimacy of your children? No, neither in civil nor canon law. It is always assumed you had what is called a "putative marriage," that is, a presumed or reputed marriage, and that is all that is required for the legitimacy of children. An annulment looks at the spiritual aspects of the marriage, not the civil, legal aspects that make children legitimate. An annulment does not change the status of a past marriage, so it is not like a divorce. It is only a discovery process to determine whether or not the marriage was invalid from the beginning. Thus, the key in determining whether an annulment is granted is the situation at the time of the marriage.

Summing It Up

To favor your chances of success in marriage, try friendship dating for the first few months of a relationship. If you're really not close to being ready for marriage, just pursue friendship dating until you are ready. Move slowly, and aim for a two-year courtship. Avoid over-dating. Try not to look upon a date in terms of personal "satisfaction." Don't live together or stay together, chastely or not. Don't buy a house together or give expensive gifts. Think of 28 as an ideal age for marriage. Be open to future Christian marriage counseling especially if you marry over thirty. Men, get a job. And if you have been married before, refrain from entering into courtship until your previous marriage has been annulled. If you keep all these things in mind, and try to follow through on them in your courtship, you will avoid a good number of marital problems in the future as well as set a good example for others.

Endnotes

1.   Some are horrified at the prospect of going out with several different people when you are first getting to know someone. They consider it "two-timing." But, this is part of the sad Western pattern of rushing into an intense courtship from the very start. Fifty years ago people didn't do that. They went out with lots of different people for a time until they decided to enter into a courtship with one of them. That is a far more reasonable approach.

2.   Connie Marshner, "Contemporary Dating as Serial Monogamy," *Homiletics and Pastoral Review*, October 1998, pp. 18–25.

3.   Kelly Grover, et al., "Mate Selection Processes and Marital Satisfaction," *Family Relations*, vol. 34, 1985, pp. 383–386. As found in Neil Clark Warren, *Finding The Love of Your Life*, New York: Simon and Schuster, 1992, *Finding The Love of Your Life*, p. 9.

4.   *CL Family Foundations*, March–April 2001, (the Couple to Couple League), p. 20.

5.   Why is reading the saints important? Because they were experts at humility, a key ingredient for good relationships. And, something not unrelated, they knew they had to die to self to love God and others. Dying to self is another key element in marriage.

6.   Neil Clark Warren, *Finding The Love of Your Life*, p. 11.

7.   Warren, *Finding The Love of Your Life*, p. 12.

8.   Tom Lasswell and Marcia Lasswell, *Marriage and The Family*, Belmont, CA: Wadsworth Publishing Co., 1987; as found in Warren, *Finding The Love of Your Life*, p. 13.

9.   Are these ages culturally conditioned? Absolutely. If we were to return to a predominantly Christian society, the ages could come down. Biology seems to invite younger marriage ages. However, it appears certain that with the great need for education in our highly technical society, we will never go back to the younger marriage ages prevalent in the agrarian culture (unless some catastrophe occurs to bring us back to that). To those who claim that they *have* been raised in a Christian subculture, I would respond, if you were spared television, if you were home-schooled, if you attended a very Catholic college, and if you are versed in the saints, you might well be an exception.

Chapter Nine

Finding Mr. Right

Some people believe that instead of being too active in seeking the right spouse you should just wait on God. That sounded good to me at first, but the more I thought about it, the more I realized God has given us certain abilities and he wants us to cooperate with him in pursuing goals by using those abilities. The key to Christian activity is this: *Pray as if everything depends on God, and work as if everything depends on you.*

On the other hand, it is dangerous to try to be too much in control in this process. You do your part by doing the right things and being in the right places, but ultimately you must wait on God to provide the right person at the right time. Trust is essential to the single person seeking marriage.

It's unfortunate that women must be so active nowadays in this process of finding the right man. It didn't used to be so. A woman used to be able to simply live her life, and a good man would come along. There were lots of activities in the churches and ample opportunities to meet a good, religious spouse. The sexual revolution has changed all that. Add to that the fact that so many people come from dysfunctional families and the pickings get slimmer and slimmer. Women have to be more active about finding the right man than ever before.

One thing most people know is that bars and dancing clubs are just about the worst places possible to meet a good, Christian spouse.[1] Nonetheless, there are ways. Launching a good search campaign is about as enjoyable as looking for a job: It's a pain. But, in many cases it has been quite successful, so it is worth doing.

Plan of Action

The first thing to do is develop a plan. In other words you should have some principles by which you are going to find, attract, and be won by Mr. Right. I would propose the following:[2]

- Commit to living real, Christian chastity, no matter what happens, regardless of what you have done in the past. No exceptions, period. Compromise only brings misery.
- Take care of yourself physically, spiritually, and mentally. Eat right, get your sleep, get plenty of exercise, and drink very little alcohol. Practice a regular prayer routine and have some real fun every week.
- Develop a positive Christian outlook toward life, and project that in your relationships, knowing that such an attitude makes you more attractive.
- Take charge of your social life; don't simply take what comes. Develop your own schedule for socializing and keep to it.
- Take charge of your dealings with men. Don't presume you must settle. Tell the men politely what you like and what you don't like.

- Be polite always, with everyone, and show real Christian patience with all.
- End relationships that are going nowhere. (This is a big one.)

We've spoken enough on chastity I think, so let's move to principle number two.

Take Care of Yourself

If you really want to find a good husband, you have to be the kind of person someone would want to marry. In other words, you have to be a good candidate yourself. Your religious commitment should be a real plus for any good Catholic man, but you want to take care of your health by eating right and getting enough rest and exercise to be fit. This will not only make you look better, but it will make you *feel* better, and give you a great outlook on life.[3]

Read good books about decent people who are well-known. Read good news magazines, read the newspaper, read a good Catholic periodical. Keep on top of what is happening in the world, so that you will have something to say when you go out.

Whenever you go out for any reason, look your best. Dress neatly with simple, becoming jewelry. Always have good posture and carry yourself with confidence. You want to always look sharp, but not seductive.

Positive Attitude[4]

If you are a dedicated Christian woman, praying daily, and reading good books, you will most likely be very positive about life. One of the saddest things to see is people who are trying to be religious fall into a negativism about the world. Sure, there are lots of bad things in our world, and people doing some terrible things, but there are many good things as well. Our outlook on life often depends on which of these we think more about. If you dwell on all the negatives of the world, your city, politics, the Church, you can become a very sour person in a short span of time.

This is not to say you can't identify things that are bad. It can be quite helpful to do so, but do it in a moderate way, and then move on to something positive. For example, if a certain politician does something wrong, rather than saying, "He is a shameful, despicable man," say something like, "He's been a big disappointment," or "He leaves a lot to be desired." The other person will get the message and you will maintain your peace, your joy. Why should you let the evil one get to you with his accomplishments? You are headed for the Kingdom, and that should put a constant smile on your face.

Taking Charge of Your Schedule

Taking charge of your schedule simply means that you are going to be in places where it is possible, even likely, that you will find a good man. The first thing to do is decide how much time you want to spend on finding the right man. It should be one or two nights a week if you really want things to happen. You can use that time for filling out applications for an online dating service, or for composing an ad, or going to an event, but as Winnefred Cutler says, you need to develop real discipline in pursuing your goal.

Taking Charge of Your Relationships

Taking charge of your relationships requires real courage. If you want to have a good marriage, *you* must set the agenda for the courtship, not only by the places you go, or the things you do, but also by insisting on the proper treatment every woman deserves.[5]

You must confide everything to the Lord, and then never fear insisting on being treated well. You don't have to be rude when you insist on respectful treatment. You can use a sense of humor, and you may have to wait for a more private situation to talk to him about certain issues. But, you need to do it, or you'll be a miserable woman all your life.

If a man just won't pick up on the behavior thing, you need to tell him goodbye, nicely, and tell him why. Perhaps you'll plant a seed that will help him reform and become a good husband for someone else.

Be Polite[6]

Just because you're going to be tough, doesn't mean you have to be rough. In other words, to succeed at finding a good husband you must know exactly what you want and be strong in holding out for it, but you must always be a lady. No one should ever cause you to lose your cool or say nasty words. That will set you back in courtship and in the spiritual life as well. You must always treat others with dignity not because they deserve it, but because you are a Christian. Christians should see the dignity in every human person. That is the foundation of the Church's social teaching, and the teaching on marriage and sexuality as well.

If you have had a foul mouth in the past, get rid of it fast. Make yourself pay big fines (send the money to the poor) if you fall back into foul language, until you have purged such words even from your thoughts. Never let a man hear you say a foul word. If you do, his respect will fall rapidly. In fact, it would be good if God never heard you say a foul word!

The rehabilitation of courtship is all about respect. Respect every man, even the most shameful liar, and act in a respectable way. You will win the esteem of every man you come across and you'll raise the bar for men with other women.

End Bad Relationships[7]

One of the hardest things for a woman to do is to end a relationship which is pleasant, but not going anywhere. One woman dated a man for seven years, from the time she was 34 until she was 40. The man was divorced, or so he said, but he didn't have an annulment. Instead of insisting he get one, she "hung on," hoping for a miracle. She was attractive, bright, and articulate but she was foolish. The man was never going to marry her. Finally, he died in an accident, and she learned that he had another girlfriend.

Ladies, you don't have to settle! Pray hard, and remind yourself over and over about a bad relationship, "This isn't going anywhere. I have to be firm and walk." Then do it. Don't worry. God will help you find someone else.

Single Catholics Online

Dating services used to be the creepiest way to find anyone, but the internet has changed things. Some great marriages are coming out of the single Catholics web sites. I have seen them happen, I've been to the weddings. It's real and it's working. Online dating can be good if you are careful and take your time.

If you decide to do this, sit down at your computer and search for "on-line Catholic dating." You should find at least two or three that meet your requirements. If I were launching a campaign to meet a good Catholic, I'd probably use at least two. If you like a site, sign up right away. Don't wait. Make it clear what you are looking for. Don't worry so much about meeting someone in your geographical area. Be flexible on the non-essentials.

Some women tell me they get lots of responses and others fewer, but it's a good place to start. Generally it's a good idea to correspond by email for a while, until you have a feeling that this is someone you click with. Then he should volunteer to call. If time drags on and he doesn't ask if he may call, you might want to say something like, "Perhaps we should talk some time." If he doesn't pick up on that and ask if he might call you, then forget him. Some people just like to send emails.

What if you are already speaking by phone to one man and you receive some interesting emails from others? Should you tell them forget it? Not at all. Only when you commit to be courted exclusively by one man should you exclude others. Keep chatting with the others and even allow them to call you too. In fact, you could have a date with one on one weekend, and another on another. Until you commit, you're not committed, so you may as well enjoy a little variety until you narrow it down to one.

What if you meet a man on one of these services who lives far away and he invites you to come and visit? Don't go. As a woman all alone in a city you don't know you would be at a great disadvantage. If he is interested, he can come and visit you. Once you have spent some time with him and are certain he is okay, you might visit him, but he should find you a place in a good family or a re-treat house, or something similar. Hotels should be avoided.

What if you have been seeing a man for several months and he invites you to move to his city? Unless you have family there forget it. Imagine how you'd feel if you moved there and things didn't work out. You'd be all alone in a new city with few friends, and goodness knows what kind of a job. If you marry, then you can move.

Personal Ads

Many people use personal ads in periodicals or newspapers as well. One of our St. Catherine Society ladies placed an ad in a paper. She discussed it with her priest before submitting it, and he had several suggestions. She met several men and ended up marrying one of them.

If you decide to place an ad in a magazine or newspaper, be sure to choose a reputable one. You can go to the library if necessary to review the periodicals and discover if they accept personals. In any event, you, as a woman, should have a post office box to which a man may write. Privacy is key here. Renting your own mailbox rather than having the magazine or paper provide one is a pain, but it's usually less expensive, and it gives you more control. You could also have him respond by email. If you do that, be sure to get an untraceable e-mail address from Juno or Yahoo and don't reveal your full name in the email address.[8]

What you write, of course, is most important. Make it clear what you want. Here's an example:

Vibrant, attractive, dedicated Catholic woman, 31-year-old, 5' 6", regular jogger, prays and attends Mass daily. Seeking practicing Catholic man with interest in spiritual growth and who knows how to have good, clean fun. Please write Box 111, etc.

You may want to be even more specific with regard to chastity right from the start. For example, your ad might read like this:

Attractive, devout Catholic woman, 5' 9", 26, seeks like-minded Catholic man, who believes in prayer, chastity and spiritual growth; and who knows how to enjoy life in a Christian way. Please write Box 222, etc.

Use your own words, but be specific enough so that you won't have to worry about the basics. One woman placed ads in four different places and had 400 responses.[9] Since you are limiting your audience to practicing Catholics, the number should be lower, but even a few could be interesting.

Winnefred Cutler makes a great observation about this process: "Don't think of the ad as the desperate search for the love of your life. Rather think of it as one of your playgrounds and get ready to enjoy yourself." She was not implying that you should take the respondents lightly, only that you don't want to obsess over them. You are the prize and you should be ready to go out with a good number of men until you find one you like. The more you go out with different men, the more your confidence will rise. Your confidence is very important in this whole courtship thing.

When you get the letters or emails, decide which ones you will respond to and place them in some sort of file. For security reasons, it's probably better for you to call him at first. If you write back, send a picture. For most men this is quite important. In any case, when you write back, don't give your address. Instead suggest he send you a note with his phone number on it to the P.O. box. With-hold your last name, address, and phone number until you are con-vinced he is safe. You may even want to exchange several letters and/or phone calls before you meet.

You need to have a good long phone conversation before you decide he is okay. And, what if he is not what you're looking for? Act decisively and make it clear that things are not going to work out. For example, "It was so nice of you to call. After talking to you I'm convinced it would not be a good idea for us to meet. I wish you the best of luck. Thanks again. Good night." Too often women are so concerned about a man's feelings that they drag out this process of ending things to the point where he gets more hurt. Just be very polite and very firm and don't wait for his response.

If he wants to meet you and you are game, agree to meet in a certain place for coffee or whatever. Again, by doing this you are protecting yourself. You need to meet him and talk to him in person before you decide if he should have your phone number and address. What if he presses you on the phone to give him your number? Simply say something like, "I don't give that until I know someone a little better." If he pushes further, just say you are getting very uncomfortable with this conversation and if he doesn't back off big time, say you've had enough and you are about to hang up. Then hang up. Caller ID can compromise this, but you can turn off your caller ID or you can use a cell phone which won't reveal your location. The potential for personal ads is great, especially if you narrow your search by the wording of your ad. Make it clear you are looking for a practicing Catholic and then be prepared for some non-practicing Catholics to reply. You will have to do further screening when you get the responses

Catholic Lectures

Catholic lectures are some of the best places to meet good Catholics. One program that has been catching on all across the USA is "Theology on Tap," lectures on the faith given in pubs. This originated in Chicago and the name is copyrighted to ensure that only orthodox speakers will give presentations. In Washington, DC literally hundreds of young people attend these events. If they have them in your area, attend.

So what happens if you show up at one of these events and you see someone you like? The best thing to do is simply smile warmly. Then look away. If the man is interested and has any self-confidence, he'll pick up on that and come over to introduce himself. If he doesn't that night, perhaps he will some other night.

You should look upon these lectures as a long-term commitment. Try to go to several in a row. That way you'll begin to get to know some people just by seeing them over and over. Sometimes a man will only approach a woman if he has seen her more than once.

At events like this, you can be a bit more relaxed about giving your phone number. Generally those who frequent these things are safe. Nonetheless, you don't want to be rushed. If a man comes up to you and introduces himself, and then right away asks for your number, you might want to say, "Wow, that was fast. Could we talk a bit first?" If he doesn't want to bother with that, even if you think he's delightful, say, "Well, perhaps we'll have another opportunity to talk," and don't give him your number. The last person you want to get involved with is a pushy man.

And, as we said earlier, you don't want to be desperate. If you're going to be the prize, you need to act like one, and not accept bad behavior. Have your standards and stick to them.

Classy men will live up to them. The others will depart. Remember, women who graciously and politely insist on good behavior will get it.

What happens if you turn a man down at an event and you see him at the next event. How can you be a Christian without encouraging him to try again? You simply smile reservedly, never warmly. You may wish him well in every way, but you don't want to give him any ideas about you. One evening one of our young women walked into a room before I was to give a talk and a young man who had made himself very unpopular with virtually every woman there caught her eye. She had met him before and, being a nice Christian woman, she smiled warmly at him. He immediately went up to her, thinking no doubt, "Maybe she likes me now." Not so.

When I talked to her later, I asked her, "Are you interested in him?"

"Of course not," she replied.

"Then tone down the smile. I thought you were egging him on."

Ladies, please, if you don't want to be pursued by a man whom you know, smile reservedly, no more. A warm smile is an important message-sender in a social situation.

When you're not interested, please make it clear. Just about every man wants a woman who is not interested to tell him so, early and directly. Say something like, "You know, I think you're very nice, but I don't think we're meant for each other." If he persists at this point, get even more direct: "I really don't want to go out with you."

What if a guy you like asks you out and you already have plans? Then just say, "I'm sorry. I already have plans Saturday. Perhaps another night?" Don't recommend which night unless he asks. In general, it's his job to propose a night. By suggesting he try some other night, you are making it clear you are interested. If he has anything on the ball, he'll come up with another plan on the spot.

Dinner Parties

Our culture has lost the art of putting on dinner parties for single friends. This is a wonderfully civilized way to meet people and really get to know them. When you are at a table with six or eight people, discussing the issues of the day, you find out a good deal about each person in a short amount of time. The woman who gives the party will not generally meet someone new at such an event, since she has to know them to invite them. An exception to that rule would be for her to include a man she likes but has never gotten to know. Or, she might invite three girlfriends on the condition that they each invite a good (Catholic) man in whom they have no romantic interest. In any event, by having dinner parties herself, perhaps her friends will follow suit, and invite her to their dinner parties.

Other Likely Places

If you get invited by a good Catholic to a wedding, or a party at their house, be sure to go. Often like-minded people will attend. Go alone to these events. That way you are much more approachable.[10]

There are any number of other events where you might meet a good Catholic man, such as pro-life events, Bible studies or prayer groups. The situation at such events would be similar to that at a good Catholic wedding or party.

Other activities, more secular in nature, such as swing dancing, tennis lessons, political groups, charity groups, and so on, have potential, but clearly not as much. These will not be as focused as some of the above, so you'll have to do some sorting out right away in these situations. And, although these activities will not be as rich in the type of men you may be seeking, they are enjoyable activities. So, it's good to do them without thinking of finding someone special. If you do, enjoy the surprise.

Is This Guy Religious?

If you do meet someone at a secular event, it may take some time to discover if he is religious, but you can ask certain questions to get some early clues. For example, "What are your main interests in life?" or "What things are most important to you?" If he asks "What do you mean?" you could answer, "Well, for example, your work, or your faith, or sports, or hiking, or reading?" If he says "It's my stamp collection," you have a major insight.

Another way is to talk freely and naturally about your own religious activities, and see how he reacts. If he never responds, he may not be interested in such things. Again, it's just early clues you are getting at this point. To really discover a man's religious commitment and potential can take several months, especially if he's a "pleaser." As I mentioned earlier, if you make it clear that you are religious and ask your date if he is, he will often say "Very," even if he hasn't been in a church for decades. So, asking directly is usually of little help.

Waiting on the Lord

Even though you are taking more control of things, you are never completely in control. God is. Do some of these things to give yourself a good chance to find Mr. Right. But, don't obsess over it! Once you've done your part, the rest is up to God.

What happens if you try some of these methods and nothing seems to come of it? Go to God in prayer and trust his timetable, which is almost always slower than our own. Keep on trying. Psalm 38 provides the key:

> Lord, all my longing is known to thee,
> my sighing is not hidden from thee.
> My heart throbs, my strength fails me;
> and the light of my eyes — it also has gone from me . . .
> But for you, O Lord, do I wait;
> it is you, O Lord my God,
> who will answer.

Summing It Up

It's important that women take charge of their social lives, and have a plan to find the right man. This means taking care of spiritual, physical, and psychological health. Be a positive person. Establish a schedule and exercise real discipline to carry out your plan. Insist on proper treatment, and always deal politely with others. Quickly end bad relationships. Pursue online Catholic dating if you will, and personal ads. Go to good Catholic lectures, weddings, and other Catholic events. Participate in enjoyable, wholesome activities. And, leave the rest up to God. He has a plan for you.

Endnotes

1. Someone will sometimes pipe up, "Not so, Father. My sister met a really great guy at a pub. He's a wonderful husband

and father." That's like saying, "My sister won the lottery. You can too." Sure, I can. But what are my chances?

2. These are based in part on principle numbers 4, 5, 8, 9 and 11 of Winnefred Cutler's eleven principles of "The Code of Courtship" in *Searching for Courtship: The Smart Woman's Guide to Finding A Good Husband,* New York: Villard Books (Div. of Random House), 1998, pp. 37–39. There is a lot of valuable advice in this book in the first seven chapters. This, despite her acceptance of pre-marital sex.

3. See Winnefred Cutler, *Searching for Courtship,* pp. 75–77.

4. See Cutler, pp. 38, 39.

5. See Cutler, pp. 31, 46, 47, 187.

6. See Cutler, pp. 38, and chapters 2 and 6 for more examples.

7. See Cutler, pp. 72–75.

8. See Cutler, pp. 176, 177.

9. See Cutler, p. 133.

10. See Cutler, p. 145.

Chapter Ten

Finding Miss Right

The task of a man finding the right person to marry is a bit different than that of a woman. A woman has to put herself in the right places to receive attention from a good man. A man has to go to the same places and find a good woman. Before speaking of the "places," let's talk briefly about the "pursuit."

'Cherchez La Femme!'

In "The Biblical Roles of Courtship" the pattern for courtship, based on Scripture and contemporary psychology, we tried to show that the man is to "pursue" the woman as his "prize." But with the ill-fated feminist revolution[1] only just beginning to die a natural death, many men are afraid to push too actively, perhaps because they don't know what to expect from women.

Men, believe me when I tell you, real Christian women are delighted to have men they like take more initiative in courtship. A healthy sensitivity as to whether or not the women are interested is always in order, but if they're interested, they want you to make the first moves.

Part of the problem may also be the fact that the whole "dating scene" has become so terribly messed up. Some Christian men are a bit shy to energetically approach women lest they be seen as part of the clingy dating scene, which is acknowledged as a failure. So, they try to get to know women by seeing them at several events before being forthright. The women are underjoyed at this approach.

If you like a woman, you don't have to pursue her like a drooling dog. Just approach her in what we earlier called "friendship dating." In other words, take the initiative, but as a friend first. Friends don't wait until there's a party to see each other. They call each other and do things together because they enjoy it. You needn't commit to courtship to go out with a woman and get to know her as a friend.

If you're interested in a woman, go ahead and invite her out for dinner or for biking or whatever. Just because you are taking the friendship dating approach doesn't mean you don't give her real attention and make it quite clear you are interested. You "pursue" her in moderation, as a friend, not as a romantic partner, for a month or two. But you *do* "pursue" her.

On October 12, 2001, just a month after the 9/11 attack Peggy Noonan wrote an editorial in the *Wall Street Journal* entitled, "Welcome Back, Duke." Her point was that after 9/11 there has arisen a new appreciation for the John Wayne type of man, who is not some effete comedian, but a man who can go out and get things done. The firemen, the policemen in New York, the ordinary working guys who make life easier for lots and lots of people are all unsung heroes. "The Duke is back," she says, "and none too soon."

The return of manliness will bring a return of gentlemanliness, for a simple reason: masculine men are almost by definition gentlemen. Example: If you're a woman and you go to a faculty meeting at an Ivy League University you'll have to fight with a male intellectual for a chair, but I assure you that if you go to a Knights of Columbus Hall, the men inside (cops, firemen, insurance agents) will rise to offer you a seat. Because they are manly men, and gentlemen.

She also praises the businessmen on flight 93 who said goodbye to their loved ones, closed up their cell phones and said, "Let's roll."

All of this applies to the man who wants to win the heart of his fair maiden. Gentlemen, now is the time to "pursue" women, not boorishly, or lustfully, or in a macho way, but as a gentleman. To be sure, a gentleman is careful to listen and watch for clear signals that she is not interested. And if she doesn't give clear signals (shame on her!) he's smart enough to ask her directly, if she's not interested. Nonetheless, men, barring her lack of interest and with friendship dating well in mind, it's time to say, "Let's roll."

The Christian Man

Before finding Miss Right, men need to *be* Mr. Right. If you hope to succeed in courtship and marriage (as well as in getting to the Kingdom), you need to pray a good deal. You should be a witness to the value of prayer. Be willing to tell others how prayer has helped you. And don't be wimpy about it.

Certainly it's also important to know the faith, especially with regard to chastity, and you shouldn't apologize for living it. Remember, the reason Christ expects chastity is because it leads to happiness. I've met many men who pretend to be Christian, but don't even try for chastity. You can't have it both ways. If you want to be a true Christian, you must at least try.

The Christian man is decisive, but gentle at the same time. Jesus is his model. He has self-confidence, but he is humble. He knows his own limitations. He holds women in high esteem and works at being polite. He is willing to lead in the faith. He uses his gifts for God, whether it be athletic talent, artistic talent, musical, or whatever. Finally, he has a full life apart from courtship, a life that is very much involved with his Church. This man is for the true Christian woman, the proverbial "good catch."

Where to Look

Online dating services can be as good a place for Christian men to meet good women as vice versa. Often men will complain, "But Father, aren't these things for losers?" They used to be, but not any more. I have seen a number of attractive, sharp Catholics find good spouses on these services. You can go to the web site and see faces along with some personal information even before you contact someone. You simply go to a search engine and look for "Catholic Dating Service" and join one or more groups. Then you go through the files until you find someone who looks interesting. Then you email her and begin the ball rolling. You exchange emails for a while, then phone calls. If all goes well, you ask if you may visit her, or, if she lives nearby, you ask her for a date. Sometimes the participants live far away from each other, but often something can be worked out. The rest us up to you.

What about placing a periodical ad for a nice, Catholic woman? It couldn't hurt but I have never heard of a man finding a woman by placing an ad. However, I have heard of some women who have met good husbands by placing a personal ad in a newspaper or periodical. So, although it might be a waste to place your own personal ad, it could be worthwhile to look through the women's ads from time to time.

One of the best places for men and women to meet is, as mentioned before, at a Catholic lecture on the faith. Some cities have "Catholic Forums" which meet periodically, others have "Theology on Tap." The latter events take place at a bar, and draw as many as 400 people for a talk on some aspect of the faith. Because the purpose is to learn, it attracts people who might not otherwise attend a singles activity. These things seem to naturally weed out the superficial Catholics.

So, you arrive at one of these events and you see a woman who looks nice. How do you proceed? The direct method work bests. You smile at her, and if she smiles too, you simply go up and say, "My name is Polycarp Snodgrass. What's yours?" The key here is to have a gentlemanly attitude, humble, and attentive to her responses. If she's interested, she'll tell you at least her first name. Repeat it, and memorize it.

Then you should have a whole list of simple, direct questions to ask, such as, "Do you work (or live) nearby?" or "Have you been to these talks before?" or "Where are you from?" Nothing too smooth or probing. Women prefer sincerity to cleverness at the start. You should appear interested but not desperate. If the conversation goes well, you can ask, "May I call you some time?" You can take it from there.

Catholic weddings can be another place to meet good people. The approach is basically the same, but somewhat easier since you have something in common: the person who invited you. Thus, you have a starting point for the conversation. (For example, "Are you a friend of Anastasia or Ambrose?")

Pro-life events are another great place to find strong Catholics. Also, prayer groups, Bible studies, and political groups that are on the correct side of moral issues. Other activities such as swing dancing, skiing, tennis, or cycling might put you in the right place to meet someone appropriate. Of course, the person you meet may not be a Catholic. Unfortunately, many good Catholics want to meet a Catholic, but they end up settling for less with catastrophic results.

Finally, dinner parties are a great way to meet people. If you host a few, your friends may reciprocate. A dinner party with six or eight people present is a dignified and personal way to get to know people. If you decide to host a large party, play some games. Two of the best games for parties are charades and Balderdash, a word bluffing game. The best arrangement is to play the game for an hour or two early in the evening, and then let people mix after that.

Asking Her Out

When it comes time to ask a woman out, don't be vague and say something like, "Would you like to go out with me Saturday night?" One of my savvy nieces got such an invitation from a guy. She asked him to be more specific, and he couldn't. So she said, "Call me when you have a plan."

Gentlemen, you *do* need a plan. When you ask a girl out, it should be for something specific, such as dinner, or dancing, or a concert, or a basketball game. Never start out with, "Would you like to get together for a date some time?" If you suggest two different nights, and her response to both is, "I'm sorry, I already have plans," then you can ask a more general question, such as, "I'm not doing so well here. Are there any days when I might have more success?" Hopefully, if she doesn't want to go out with you, she'll tell you so, politely but directly, at this point.

Men, you have to try if you want to succeed. If you like a woman, and she likes you, go out, slay the dragon, and win her heart. Don't be like the guy who dated a young woman who was so taken with him she told her parents, "Now there's a guy I could marry!" Her parents didn't like him because he was eight years older than she. She was foolish enough to allow them to influence her. I asked him, "Well, do you like her a lot?"

"Sure," he said.

"Then what are you going to do about it?" I continued.

"Well, she seems to be going along with her parents. I'm going to give up."

"Are you serious?" I asked. "Why not offer to go with her to visit her parents and at least meet them. Let them see who you are. Maybe then they'll change their mind." He wouldn't hear of it. Who knows what might have happened if he had persisted?

Of course, no one likes to be rejected, but part of being a man is dealing with rejection. It goes with the territory. As men, we are supposed to be able to handle it. That's why the man asks the woman out, so he can deal with being turned down. Men are supposed to be tougher about such things. So, you try and you fail. So what? Get up and try again.

It seems that too many men today are suffering from "wimplash." Remember, faint heart ne'er won fair maiden.

Romance

The man is supposed to provide most of the romance in a courtship. What exactly do we mean by romance? An adventurous, heroic or creative way of pursuing a woman; a colorful or imaginative way of protesting one's love. Women always like a little color, variety, pizzazz. We men are often not into that. So, romance is a way of saying to the woman, "You inspire me to be creative, to be innovative."

What are some ways of being romantic with your sweetheart? Bring her a rose, or at least a flower, when you go to pick her up for a date. Women love flowers. Sometimes even schmaltzy ideas can work well. One Christmas, a very creative and romantic guy decided to make a pedestal for his sweetheart. He took a block of wood, etched the name of his girl on top, wrote a poem and presented it to her. She was delighted.

Actually, the poetry was probably the thing that moved her most. Poetry is a big hit with most women. My brother-in-law used to send my sister passages from Cyrano de Bergerac, for instance. If you can make up your own poetry, go for it. It doesn't have to be polished, just sincere.

One guy wrote to his sweetheart:

> If we were to marry in time to come,
> For me to stop courting would be awful dumb.
> For you I'd take the garbage out,
> And help you wash the shirts.
> Isn't that what love's about,
> Just giving when it hurts?
> With even five kids
> I'd still send you roses
> To full up your hearts
> And fill up your noses.

Notice that the man clearly states his love, but he includes somewhat klutzy humor. His girlfriend said that she found such poetry "sweet." If you can't create your own verse, try Cyrano.

Little cards sent from time to time are often a big hit. You can get one at the card shop, or make one up. With computers, you can really do something funny and personal.

Finally, if you can come up with a really creative idea, it may just be the ticket. One day I was at the beach and a boat came by. It was moving very slowly and the man in the boat had a big sign. It read, "Felicity, will you marry me?" Felicity was sitting on the beach with her boyfriend and a bunch of other friends. He had the ring all ready. Apparently she said yes because twenty minutes later the boat returned with another sign: "Happy day! She said yes!"

If you're going to ask a woman on a date, try to be creative and romantic. One good book for ideas is *Cheap Dates: Fun, Creative and Romantic Dates that Won't Break Your Budget* by Steven C. Smith. The emphasis is not on cheap, despite the title. Warning: if you do buy the book, you might want to either remove the cover, or put tape over it. If your sweetheart sees that title, you're a dead duck! The following are a few suggestions for romantic dates, based on the book.

Some of the most romantic dates are picnics. Go to a nice deli and get some exotic dishes. Bring a nice clean blanket (the beach blanket you haven't washed for five years won't do) and find a good park where you can spread out the blanket and have some space to yourselves. Don't forget a rose in a vase. This is a great setting for intimate bonding.

Watching the sun rise together is another romantic date. Or, so I thought in my senior year of college. I told my date I'd be at her dorm by 5:30 a.m. (which shows abundantly how much

I loved her). I reminded her to set her alarm because, in those days, men weren't allowed in women's dorms. I was there at 5:30 a.m. When she didn't arrive after fifteen minutes, I risked the wrath of everyone on her corridor and called her on the house phone. The woman who answered the phone clearly was not happy. "Do you know what time it is?" she said as she slammed down the phone.

Next I tried little pebbles on the window. After three or four shots, a kindly coed comes to the window. I tell her I have a date with my girlfriend to watch the sun rise. "I'll get her," she answers. (I should say a Mass for that woman some day.)

Five minutes later my date walks out of the dorm, we get to our viewing place and watch the sun come up. It was a great date. If you should try this, call on her cell phone. If she doesn't have one, lend her yours! Hell hath no fury like a corridor mate awakened at 5:45 a.m!

Another romantic adventure is a ride through the park in a horse-drawn carriage. Or a walk around the lake at sunset (if neither of you are into sunrises). Or a trip to the ice cream parlor to have one big ice cream soda, with two straws.

Eating outside is always romantic. Barbecue some steaks on the grill, and set up a table with tablecloth and candlelight outside on the patio. (Be sure to spray the place for bugs beforehand.) For an added touch, use a portable CD player for mood music. Of course, if you have a musical friend who owes you a favor, you could have him serenade the two of you! Some of the most beautiful views can be found in rooftop restaurants. If the menu is affordable, go for it. If not, be not afraid. Go to a nice restaurant for dinner, and then take her to the rooftop site for dessert.

Another great date is to take a walk on the beach at sunset. Roll up your pantlegs and walk barefoot in the surf. Have a fireplace? Move the couch in front of it, build a big, roaring fire and talk.

These should at least get you started thinking about romantic dates. Remember too, there are plenty of other types of dates besides romantic ones. Movies, plays, concerts, hiking, boating, fishing (if she is into it), lectures (religious or not), board games . . . to name just a few.

By the way, Christian women don't necessarily want men to spend a lot of money on them, but they want *creativity*. If your girlfriend complains that you don't take her out much anymore, bringing her to a family restaurant for an evening of dining probably isn't going to help your cause. It doesn't have to be the Ritz, but it should have some character.

Summing It Up

The first challenge is to be willing to pursue the woman with great energy once he knows she's interested. And, he should be a good catch — that is, a well-rounded Christian man, knowledgeable about the faith, unafraid to speak about it, and proud to live it.

To find Miss Right, try the online services, good Catholic talks, and dinner parties, or any parties, especially those given by solid Catholics. Certainly weddings, and pro-life events, prayer groups, Bible studies and Catholic-friendly political groups can also be worthwhile. Dancing and sporting activities, and even blind dates can be good as well. When you find someone nice, call her with a plan, and pursue friendship dating at first, but do *pursue*. And, finally, when you get into courtship, be creative. Tell her you love her in imaginative, romantic ways. *Viva l'amour!*

Endnotes

1. Some feminist goals were great, for example, equal pay for equal work. But when they started to insist on being just like men, they shot themselves in the foot. They ruined a great thing: femininity.

Chapter Eleven

Communications 101

Why is communication so difficult between men and women? Because, as John Gray wrote in his best-selling book, *Men Are from Mars, Women Are from Venus*. In other words, men think one way, women another. In communication between the sexes, adaptability is the name of the game. He needs to understand how she thinks, and she needs to understand how he thinks. Then each can adapt to the other.

In the past twenty-plus years I have listened to many couples, some married, some single, tell of their relationship woes, and the scenario is the same 80 percent of the time. First, the man does something wrong: he forgets an anniversary or a birthday; he is too familiar with an old girlfriend; he failed to call his sweetheart when he was supposed to. It's not that women never do anything wrong, but most men are less sensitive to women's *faux pas*, and women, being more sensitive generally, are less likely to make one.

In any case, something happens to make a woman upset. It may not even be something the man has done, but something's bothering her emotionally. So, she gets a little angry and says, "You don't care about me."

"What do you mean by that?" he asks. He thinks he cares about her a lot. He takes her out to nice restaurants; he calls her several times a week; he goes to visit her family; he bought her a dozen roses recently. He thinks she should know he cares for her.

"You didn't call me yesterday. You knew I had that interview."

He starts to defend himself. Big mistake. "You only mentioned the interview once. I didn't think it was that big of a deal." Be careful. Little deals can become big deals if you call them little.

"Well, it was. I really needed to talk to you."

"Why didn't you call *me?*" he continues down this ruinous path of self-defense.

"I did. There was no answer. I left a message."

"Oh yeah, I got in too late to call you. Well, look, it wasn't that important, was it?"

Now she's really angry. She thinks he's trying to blow the whole thing off as trivial. It may indeed be trivial, objectively speaking, but that won't help him. The problem is her heart. She's a woman. She's very connected to her emotions. She needs to have them soothed, and he's the one to do it.

"How can you be so insensitive? You're never there when I need you. You're always doing this to me." He isn't always doing this to her and deep down she knows it, but it *feels* as if he is always doing this to her, especially right now!

"I do not *always* do this to you," he says, correctly, but foolishly.

Now she's angrier than ever. He's getting logical while she wants to be emotional. At this point, if these disagreements have gone on for a while, she may say something harsh, like, "You jerk, you just don't get it, do you!"

At this point he is totally frustrated, and he says either out loud or to himself, "What did *I* do? Women! You can't win." He just throws up his emotional hands and shuts up. He knows if he says anything he's a dead duck.

Sound familiar? The problem is, as we said earlier, men and women don't think the same way. Men are problem-oriented, or issue-oriented. Women are heart-oriented; they are not concerned about the issue but about their heart, to which they are tightly connected. In other words, the issue is often not the issue. Her *heart* is the issue. So how does he take care of her heart? And how does she help him do it?

What Mortimer Can Do

Let's start with Mortimer (let's call him). First, he has to understand how his sweetheart, Esmeralda, thinks. As John Gray points out in *Men Are from Mars, Women Are from Venus*, men tend to want to analyze and solve the problem when women are upset. Women just want to talk. They want their man to simply console them, and it's not that hard.

One woman, described in Gary Smalley's *If Only He Knew* (a book for men only), said, "If my husband would only put his arms around me and hold me, without lecturing me when I'm feeling blue."[1] Now women must realize that we men are a bit dense. One request usually won't do it.

The woman who kept getting the lectures knew that, so she persisted in saying as sweetly as possible, "Don't lecture me . . . just hold me and understand." The first six or seven times it had no effect. One day it finally penetrated. He decided to just do what she asked. He just held her. She was so responsive that he decided to keep doing it. Smalley reports that their marriage got better and better.

Remember, men, there is no need to defend yourself. Just tell her you're sorry she's feeling upset. You hate to see her hurting like that. "I'm here for you sweetheart. Your happiness is so important to me." Bingo! No solutions. No excuses. No analyses. And, no sweat! Just be there! Women say they can hardly keep from loving a man who does that. What could be simpler!

If a man learns nothing else about women he should learn this: *When your woman is upset, this is your chance to be her knight in shining armor. If you console her you will be a hero!* All the flowers you gave her last week, the effort you went to washing and waxing her car, the hundreds of dollars you may have spent on her, the love notes, the sacrifices you made are nice, but they won't win her heart. You win her heart when you're there to console her when she's upset. That's what really counts. And, to keep the love of a woman, you will have to do this several times a month. Believe me, it's a small price to pay for the peace and happiness it will bring, for the beautiful intimacy it will generate.

One devout young couple was having tremendous blowups from time to time so they came to see me. They would be at a party and he would spend too much time talking to some old friends, often ignoring his sweetheart in the process. She would get a sad look on her face and when he asked her the problem, she would tell him. He, unfortunately, would say, "You're too sensitive. It's really nothing." Not smart. She would, of course, get even more upset and World War III would often follow. This happened repeatedly, over any number of things.

One day I said to him, "Why don't you just tell her you love her, and that she's the most important person in your life." He said, "Because when she gets like that, I don't *feel* a lot of love for her.

I'm trying to be authentic." *Red alert! Red alert! Red alert! Man the battle stations!*

Men, the love you should have for your woman at all times is not a feeling, as we discussed previously. It's a concern for her good! If you will only tell your sweetheart you love her when you feel like it, you're in for a hard time with *any* woman. You must be prepared to tell your woman you love her, that her happiness is the most important thing in your life after God, anytime she needs to hear it, anytime she is feeling blue for *whatever* reason.

If you marry, there may be days, even weeks or months, when you don't feel any love for your wife. You may feel like she's your worst enemy. Yet, you must say "I love you," because you promised to "love and honor" her all the days of your life. You must say "I love you," because that will heal so many ills. You must say "I love you," because if you do so, and really work at it, you will find that feeling again. You must say I love you because so often "people need loving the most when they deserve it the least."[2]

One of the worst things a man can do is to forget about his girlfriend's heart once he gets married. "I've got her now," some think. "I don't need to court her anymore. I can relax." A man must win his wife's heart every day. It's not hard, once you get used to it and make it a habit, but it's something you must keep doing for the rest of your life. Always take her heart seriously, and always try to nourish it. If you do, you'll have a lot to smile about.

Make Her Number One

Gary Smalley had a tremendous problem in his marriage once. His wife complained that whenever they had a date planned, and something else came up, he would postpone her and do the "something else." She told him "You'd really rather be at work, or with your friends, or counseling people than spending time with me." He was, in effect, making the person who should have been the most important one in his life, feel like the least important.

He began to change, and what he wrote in *If Only He Knew* is telling:

> I *wanted* to tell her she was the most important person in my life. I really *wanted* to feel that way. At first I didn't have those feelings, but I *wanted* to have them. As I tried to make her more important to me than anyone else, I soon began to *feel* she was top priority . . . In other words, the warm inner feeling I have for Norma began to burn *after* I placed the "queen's crown" on her head.

This is key to any relationship. Feelings follow effort. If you wait for feelings to kick in before you act, you'll never be happy. Love is in the will; it's a decision. If you love your woman with your will, she will send your heart to the moon! Never forget that. The woman who receives willed love from her husband every day will make him feel like a king. And, when it comes to her physical response to him in the marital embrace, *wow*! (This, according to my best sources.)

A further lesson from the Smalley story is to *make her number one*. Never, never, never break a date with your woman for anything short of a national emergency. I was counseling a young married couple once and they had all the typical problems. They were driving each other crazy and tensions were very high when they came in. I was able to get the husband to ask his wife out on a date, something he hadn't done in a long time. She had arranged for a baby-sitter and the dinner reservations were made. Three days before his friend offered him two tickets to an NBA playoff game. Had his wife liked basketball, he could have taken her, but he knew she had no use for basketball. So, he reasoned he could go out with her any time, but tickets to a playoff are a once-in-a-lifetime opportunity.

Big mistake. Had he been loving his wife romantically, and inviting her out on a date every week, and making her feel important at every opportunity for the previous two years, he might have been able to cancel their date in favor of the basketball game. But, in his situation, he was in big trouble for even bringing it up. They went to dinner, and had a good time, but she was still stewing by the time they came to see me again.

Got a date with your woman and have a chance for tickets to the Super Bowl? Forget it! Tape it! That's what VCR's are for. Your team may achieve a glorious victory, but you will lose out. That applies to before marriage and especially after! There could be exceptions if you have treated her like a queen for a long time, but if I were you, I wouldn't risk it.

Give Her More Than a Little Respect

Never belittle her opinion about anything. You may disagree, but don't act like her opinion is worthless. Respect her at all times. This is part of honoring your woman, and when you marry, you promise to love and *honor* her all the days of your life. One couple I counseled was having a terrible time in their marriage. I asked them to whisper to each other every morning, "I will love and honor you today." Their marriage definitely improved. I suggest that starting right now you say to yourself every day, "I will love and honor my girlfriend today."

Another thing that destroys relationships is being hyper-critical. This comes up more often in marriage but it comes up in courtship as well. It's so easy to get into the habit of criticizing your sweetheart, and nothing will sour a relationship more quickly. Virtually all the books on marriage proclaim, "Stop criticizing your spouse." For those who are courting, I say, *"Don't even start!"*

Gary Smalley was watching a football game one Sunday afternoon with his family, and his wife made sandwiches for herself and the three children, but no sandwich for him. Several days later he got up the courage to ask her why. She said, "Are you serious? Do you realize that every time I make you a sandwich you say something critical about it? 'Norma, you didn't give me enough lettuce. Is this avocado ripe? You put too much mayonnaise on this.' I just wasn't up to being criticized the other day." Now he could have argued with the "every time" phrase, but he didn't. He had learned that "every time" simply means "often" when a woman is upset. After that he praised her every sandwich, and voila! He got sandwiches again.

Try a little experiment for a week: keep track of every time you criticize your sweetheart, and every time you praise her. The first number should be very low, the second high. In addition, if the ratio is not two to one or greater, it's time to reform.

Express Anger Rationally and Gently

Anger is poison to a relationship. Work very hard to get rid of all residual anger in your life. If you are angry with your sweetheart, ask yourself first of all, "Is this important?" If not, tell yourself, "Forget it. It's nothing." If it is worth mentioning, and it can help to mention it, tell her with kindness, "I'm really angry with you," and then tell her why. Or find a humorous way to tell her.

What if it won't do any good to mention it? Then don't. Offer your feelings as a sacrifice to God, and let it go. (If there are a lot of things you can't mention to your sweetheart, you should rethink the whole relationship.) In any case, you should always do something constructive with your anger. Holding it in will have a bad effect on your psyche.

Another important point: don't clam up or stop calling her for a week if you are angry. Learn to express your dissatisfaction without destroying her. Expressing anger rationally, without losing your temper, is one of the most important communication skills you will ever learn. It will not only make your courtship and marriage flourish, it will sweeten your whole life.

Once, long before I entered the seminary, the woman I was dating rushed through our goodnight with a flip comment that really made me angry. I called her the next day and asked if we could talk for a few minutes. As we discussed it, I explained to her that I was a bit hurt about what she had said the night before. I said, "I hope we don't become so familiar that we don't respect each other." She apologized, explaining that she had to get up early and was feeling rushed. It never came up again.

Many counselors recommend that you express dissatisfaction with words like, "I am feeling very insignificant right now," or "When you said I wouldn't understand, I felt hurt." Always try to express how *you* are feeling before you tell someone what *they* did. That is a good way to keep them from becoming defensive.

Another good way to defuse a situation that has the potential for trouble is to begin with a question. For example, "Do you know who told Hortens I was an ogre?" It may be that Hortens just made it all up. So, by starting with a question, you are avoiding making an accusation.

One final point. If you find all of a sudden you don't know how to make her happy anymore, *ask her what you're doing wrong,* and keep asking, and mean it. Ask her how you could have reacted in a certain situation to make her happy. Then listen carefully to what she says and do it. Write it down so you won't forget it!

What Esmeralda Can Do

Communication goes both ways, however. The woman needs to develop the skill to let her man know gently what she wants and not fly off the handle. She has to persevere gently telling her mate what she'd like. Gary Smalley tells the story of the woman who got upset because her husband spent so much time with his family. She felt he preferred them to her. He told her over and over again "You're too sensitive," or "You're overreacting." For a time they had to live apart from his family and she was hoping this would change. It didn't. There were many, many phone calls, and lots of visits. When he told her they had an opportunity to move back, she cried. He asked her why she was so upset and she told him she felt his preference for his family would come into play again, and again he defended himself. Later, while visiting his family on vacation, he asked her, "Tell me once more why you don't want to move back?" She did, and he finally got it. He began to show her priority at every opportunity, and their marriage grew better and better.

Ladies, remember one thing: we men are very thick. We just don't get it the first time. Or the second, or the third. Be patient. It's not bad will. It's thickness. Just about every man has it, so persevere in kindness. Nagging just builds resistance, so repeat and repeat again. Each time you sweetly tell him what you want, pretend it's the first time. You probably won't be disappointed.

One wife complained to me that her husband came home every night and made so much noise he woke up their sleeping children.

I suggested that she meet him at the door and remind him to be quiet so as not to wake the household. I spoke to her a few weeks later and asked if things were better. She said they were.

"Great," I said. "How many times did you have to tell him?"

"Only about four or five," she responded.

"Only four or five?" I answered. "You've got a good man there. Hang on to him!"

Playful Anger

Is there a way for a woman to get angry at her man without harshness and without setting her heart against him? Is there a way of getting angry that will amuse him rather than anger him? Absolutely. It's called "childlike anger" in Helen Andelin's best-seller, *Fascinating Womanhood*. I would call it "playful anger."

Basically, here's how it works: the woman becomes "adorably angry" as does a young child. She threatens never to speak to him again, and as she walks away she looks back to see if he is taking her seriously. This childlike exaggeration makes the man want to laugh. It makes him feel stronger, sensible, like a real man. This sauciness of a child, says Andelin, is most attractive to a man, and is far better than the harshness of an embittered woman (*or* resentful silence).[3]

Andelin's rules include:

1. Eliminate all bitterness, resentment, sarcasm, hate, and ugliness.
2. Use only adjectives which will uphold his masculinity, such as big, tough, lug, brute, hard-headed, stiff-necked, or hairy beast. Never use imp, nerd, wimp, little, creep, or jerk. It doesn't matter whether he's four-eleven or six-five, he's always "big."

3. Exaggerate. For example, "What's a big brute like you doing picking on a poor, defenseless woman like me?" Or make an exaggerated threat such as "I'll never speak to you again!"[4]

One woman Andelin describes had had a miserable marriage for eight years. She started being more positive and loving as taught in *Fascinating Womanhood*, and things improved. One day her husband was telling a young marriage-minded bachelor he should think twice before marrying. "Look at all the headaches a wife can bring." He kept going on and on, knowing she was very much within earshot.

Finally she had had enough. She decided to try playful anger. She turned to him, stomped her foot, and said, "You big hairy beast! I'm never going to like you again, ever!" As she left the room she looked back with a faint smile. Her husband was grinning from ear to ear as he said to the young man, "Did you hear what she called me?"

When she got to her bedroom she wondered, "Great, but what now?" He had never once apologized in eight years. But just minutes later he came in and said "I'm sorry and I didn't mean to hurt your feelings. Will you forgive me?" She wrote "I'd have forgiven him anything at that moment."

Two months later he gave her a birthday card — his first ever. It had a cute little hairy beast on the front, and on the inside he had written, "Happy Birthday, Lovingly, your Hairy Beast."[5]

Some single women say this playful, childlike stuff is beneath their dignity. However, most married women understand the need to defuse situations. Once a woman has been married for a while, she tends to shed her illusions of grandeur. Married life can be sobering. It calls for lots of humility. Anything that will help us become more childlike, which is a condition for entering the

Kingdom,[6] and will bring humor where there is anger, is worth considering. If there are some aspects of "playful anger" that you can't bring yourself to do, fine. Choose what you can handle, and try it.

Whatever way you choose to express anger, be sure it's rational. Try to make it sweet, and if you can, make it humorous. And try to be diplomatic. Arnold Palmer was playing in a big golf tournament years ago, and the crowd was making noise as he crouched down to putt. He stood up. I wondered how this great crowd-pleaser was going to handle this diplomatically. He opened his eyes wide, smiled and put his finger up to his mouth saying "Sh-h-h-h-h." Great move.

Finally, what can you do that expresses your displeasure without escalating things into a war? Just say, "Ouch!"[7] Leave it at that and say no more. Don't get antsy if there are a few minutes of silence. Just wait it out and see what happens.

Stop Criticizing and Don't Manipulate!

Another important thing to remember is to stop criticizing and start praising your sweetheart. Certainly this applies as much to women as to men. Don't try to change him, or control him. You may plant some seeds as to what you like, but if he doesn't respond right away, don't get manipulative. Just be patient and decide on what you can and can't accept.

One young woman who was having a terrible time in her marriage came to see me. It was clear that he was doing some things wrong and she was nagging him for it. I asked her if there were any good things he was doing. "Sure," she said.

"Have you thanked him for these things?" I asked.

"Well, no," she admitted.

I told her to go home and make a list of all the things he did for which she was thankful. Then, I suggested, she should thank him for one or two each day. She did, and soon reported things were improving.

Manipulation is another temptation. One woman tried to get her husband to join her church. She kept at it, day in and day out, but he resisted. So she arranged a sting operation with her friends at the church. They were to show up at around dinner time hoping he would invite them to stay for dinner. They brought books, tapes, videos. They arrived at just the right time and he did invite them to stay for dinner. All was proceeding according to plan.

After dinner, the wife said, "Wouldn't it be nice if these two gentlemen explained a little bit about the church." The husband was trapped. He agreed out of courtesy, but as they were setting up their materials, he excused himself and went to the bathroom. He climbed out the bathroom window and disappeared. He didn't return that night and the next day he was still missing.

The wife was beside herself and asked some men from her church to try to find him. After three days of searching they found him. He had no intention of coming back, but due to the kind words of the men and his wife's promise never to mention religion again, he returned. She kept her promise.

The husband became friends with one of the men who found him. He told his rescuer he had wanted to learn more about the church, but not from his wife. So he began to secretly study the faith and became a member. One Sunday the minister announced they had a new member in their congregation, and up walked the husband. His wife wept tears of joy. The moral of the story is: if you want your man to make a big change, don't nag him about it.[8] Shortly after being ordained I discovered that being an associate pastor has some of the disadvantages of being married. When I wanted something and really pushed the pastor for it, I never got it.

When I kept my mouth shut and waited, I got it. Once a pastor told me after he quit smoking, "If you had said one word about my smoking, I would never have stopped." I bit my tongue to keep from commenting on the illogic of that statement.

With another pastor, it was a badly needed backstop for the baseball field. My predecessor had begged the man for a backstop, but got nowhere. Knowing that, I said nothing. A month into our new parish softball league, one of our laymen said to the pastor, "Father, do you think we could put in a backstop for our softball league?" He answered, "Sure, great idea. How much will it take? Will four thousand do it?" That did it. No nagging. Backstop went in.

Sweet Love!

Mortimer Jones and Esmeralda Smith have read Gary Smalley's *If Only He Knew* and Helen Andelin's *Fascinating Womanhood* respectively, on how to communicate with each other. They have prayed for the *humility* to do what is needed. Now, how might their conversation go in the situation we considered earlier? Again, he failed to call her last night, when she was expecting it. So, the *Fascinating Woman* goes into action.

"Jones, you're in trouble." [She's letting him know she's angry but in a humorous way.]

"Who, me?" [He plays along.]

"Yep, you."

"What'd I do."

"You didn't call me last night, you big gorilla."

"Uh, oh. I messed up, didn't I? [He's been reading Smalley. No excuses this time.] Let me think for a minute here. Oh! You had that interview, didn't you?"

"Yeah, you remember now." She's starting to warm up already.

"Sweetheart, I don't know how you put up with me. I should have known you'd want to talk. [He should have known women *always* want to talk after an interview. But, he's a man, and he didn't think of it. Not so unusual.] C'mere. Let's sit down. I want to hear all about it."

"I don't know if I should tell you now. I should pound your chest first." [She's got a tiny smile on her face!]

"Go ahead. I deserve it. Go ahead. Right here."

So she does pound him a few times on the chest.

"Feel better? I don't blame you one bit for being angry. You told me about the interview, you made it clear it was on your mind, and I wasn't there for you when you needed me. Now, sweetheart, I really want to hear about how it went."

So she tells him how it went. He listens as he has never listened before. She gives him twice the details he needs, but he listens intently and even repeats her words to lead her to continue. [He's becoming a *great* conversationalist! He's listening!] She finishes and he feels it was not that momentous an event, but does he say that? No way!

"It sounds to me like you did very well. I'm proud of you," He says. She's beaming now.

Most men would just presume it was over by this point, but not Mortimer. Well, not the *new* Mortimer. He knows there is still some healing in order. He says, "Look at me. I want you to know I am really sorry I wasn't there for you. Will you forgive me?"

"Well, I might . . ."

"You know, sweetheart, sometimes we men are a little dense. [Women love to hear this self-evident truth proclaimed by their men.] I need you to coach me in the whole sensitivity area. I am really willing to learn, but I need you to help me. Tell me you will?"

"Okay, if you put it that way."
This was almost fun. Women are great!, he thinks.
She thinks, *What a man!*

It's Not Natural!

One young woman sent me an email after having read *Fascinating Womanhood* and *For Better or for Best*, complaining that it wasn't natural to act like that. She said she thought that many of the ways Andelin and Smalley suggest for a woman to act seemed "fake", and not the way she or other women would naturally act. She said she had been trying to act in those ways, but she felt she had been playing a role that was not her. She just didn't know if she could play a role for the rest of her life.

I wrote back to her as follows:

It is precisely because women do not naturally act as Andelin and Smalley suggest that their work is so important. The last thing we want to do as Christians is do what comes naturally. To become real Christians, we must discover how we can act in love, and then strive to do that, not in a way that comes naturally. What comes naturally is often what harms relationships.

You are indeed playing a role when you do the things these people suggest, the role of Christ. We must ask ourselves in every situation, "What would Jesus do?" and then try to do it. Although it is like playing a role at first, when we keep at it, it becomes a habit (a virtue is simply a good habit), and then we need not think much about it any more. It becomes second nature. Then we do these things more naturally, but they are in fact, supernatural.

People can change, but not through nagging or manipulation. What's true for the men, applies to the women. Praise much more often than you criticize. Keep count at times just to see if your praises far exceed your criticisms. Honor and respect your mate. And don't forget to keep praying.

God, Why'd You Make Us So Different?

Did you ever wonder why God made men and women so different? Why couldn't he have made us the same? It would be so much easier!

I am convinced he did it for at least two reasons. First, men and women are so different to prepare us for the encounter with God who is totally other. I have often said to married men and women, "If you think it's hard loving your spouse, wait until you try to love God. He is *really* different." Every one of us has been created to be God's spouse. Because the Lord has designed marriage to be between a man and a woman, he is, in a way, showing us that adaptability is the name of the game when it comes to love. You need to adapt yourself to your beloved. This is far more true of the divine marriage than the human. If we are to be worthy of intimacy with God we will have to turn ourselves inside out and upside down a hundred times because he is totally other! Luckily, he gives us the power (grace) to do all this if we are willing. And, of course, he gives us the grace to adapt to our spouses, if we are willing to (a) go to him for the grace, and (b) adapt our way of communicating to this person who is so different.

The second reason is that God has all the virtues we typically associate with both men and woman. When a man marries a woman, it is meant to be, in part, a learning experience. He is to learn gentleness, civilization, sensitivity, and a personal concern for others, among other things, from his wife. She, on the other hand, is to learn from him logic, discipline, self-motivation, and decisiveness. Are there exceptions, where one or the other is weak in the areas traditionally found in their gender? Sure, but by and large, these hold true. When a man or woman has all the virtues typical of their gender, and learns the others from their spouse, they become a complete Christian person. They are, at least with regard to virtue, ready for God.

Could God have endowed both men and women with the same virtues, so they would not have to learn from each other and adapt to each other? Sure, but then we'd get psychologically flabby and would have no clue as to how to prepare for the ultimate marriage, the divine one. As it is, every earthly marriage is somehow a preparation for the heavenly one.

Sure It's Hard

Changing to accommodate your sweetheart is very hard work, but worth every ounce of the effort! It's not easy to change. Pride always tries to get in the way. Pray for humility. Many couples know what to do, but haven't the humility to actually carry it out! Read about Francis of Assisi, and other humble saints. Learn the great value of humility from them. Then work very hard to change and overcome your natural inclinations. It seems harder nowadays to do these things, but it's no harder than it ever was. The reason it seems harder is that everything else has gotten so much *easier*. Much of life is far easier today than it was even 50 years ago. Not relationships. They are just as hard as they ever were.

Summing It Up

To keep peace in courtship and marriage, a man must attend to the heart and to the emotions of his woman. He must always make her number one, and never belittle her ideas. He must learn to express his anger reasonably, politely and never be too proud to ask her to coach him on how to treat her.

A woman must gently and diplomatically let her man know what she needs, especially emotionally, and be willing to tell him sweetly over and over. When she gets angry, she should express it in a child-like or playful way. She should not try to change him by negative or manipulative behavior, but encourage him so that in time he may *want* to change for the better. Both should minimize criticism and be lavish with praise.

The only thing more difficult than learning how to love your sweetheart is learning to love God. But, loving your husband or wife will prepare you for the most rewarding and hardest thing: your eternal marriage with God.

Endnotes

1. Every man who hopes to have a good marriage should read this book.

2. John Harrigan as quoted in Laura Doyle, *The Surrendered Wife*, New York: Simon and Schuster, 1999, p. 191.

3. Helen Andelin, *Fascinating Womanhood*, New York: Bantam Books, pp. 320, 321.

4. Andelin, pp. 322, 323.

5. Andelin, pp. 327–329.

6. (Jesus) called a child over, placed it in their midst, and said, "Amen, I say to you, unless you turn and become like chil-

dren, you will not enter the kingdom of heaven. Whoever humbles himself like this child is the greatest in the kingdom of heaven" (Matthew 18:2–4).

7. Laura Doyle, *The Surrendered Wife*, p. 180.

8. Andelin, p. 42.

Chapter Twelve

Past Sins and New Beginnings

Nowadays, it seems that a fair number of devout Catholic singles have committed some rather serious sins before coming back to the Lord. This raises the question of how to deal with your past once you meet someone special and marriage is a possibility.

One young Christian couple had been going out for some time, and the subject of the past came up. The girl felt she had to tell her boyfriend that she had had sex with three different men and had thought she was pregnant by one. She had gone to an abortion center and had the money with her to pay for it before one of the abortionists came in and said, "Ma'am, there's been a mistake. You're not pregnant." He told me he was able to deal with what she told him because he had worked such a possible scenario through, knowing that in a sex-soaked world there was a good chance that he might face such a situation. Nonetheless, he wondered why she had to tell him such details. Had she just said that she had made some mistakes regarding chastity he said he would have been more than satisfied.

Another situation involved a couple in which the girl had had several sexual partners before her conversion. When she told him she had not always been chaste, he began to press her for details, such as how many men, under what circumstances, etc. She asked me what to do and I told her to give no details. "Most men say they want details, but when they get them they can't deal with it." So she refused to give details, saying that if she told him anything more it would just hurt him. They eventually got married and they have a happy family.

One young woman had contracted Human Papillomavirus (HPV) in her numerous sexual adventures before she found God and began living the Gospel. She dated a man for two years before she told him that she had a sexually transmitted disease. She said she intended to tell a man only when she thought marriage was a real possibility. He didn't break up with her over this, but he was not happy that she had waited so long to tell him. He was right. When you begin a real courtship with someone, that's the time to tell something so important as this. Withholding such information could even be later grounds for an annulment.

All of this points to a crucial question: Does your sweetheart have the right to know what sins you have committed in the past? My advice is yes, if it will affect the relationship. Otherwise no. Let's consider some of the possibilities one at a time.

Sexual Sins

First, fornication (sexual activity outside of marriage) or adultery (sexual activity with someone who is married to another person). When your past comes up, you should acknowledge past sins in a general way. You could say something like, "I have not always been chaste in the past." If your sweetheart asks for more information, you could simply say, "I committed sexual sins before I began to live the faith."

What if he or she asks, "Well, I'd like to know more"? I would say, "I don't want to go into details." If they press, simply tell them, as did the woman described earlier, you're not going to give details. In every situation I have seen, giving details of past sins has caused major problems.

Should a person speak about these sins during friendship dating? I don't see why. Talking about the past should only be important when a real courtship is in progress. Friendship dating is simply aimed at seeing if you are compatible. You don't ordinarily tell your friends about your past sins so neither should you in friendship dating.

What should a woman do if a man suggests that since she has already had relations with men in the past, she should do so with him as well so as to achieve some sort of parity? Simply decline, and say something like, "I'm surprised you would suggest such a thing. I thought you were a good Christian and wanted to help me be one, too."

Venereal Disease

What if a person has a venereal disease? As mentioned before, holding back on something like this could be grounds for annulment. When does one tell his/her partner? Not during friendship dating, but early in courtship. He (let's say) needs to tell her early on so that she can make a rational decision about this *before* she gets emotionally entangled.

How would a person tell his/her sweetheart? Suppose a woman has herpes. She could say something like, "I have something to tell you which may make you want to end our relationship. I can accept that. Let me preface this by saying that I grew up without a real faith. I went along with what most of the kids were doing in high school, and in college as well. It was only four years ago that I began to understand the Catholic faith, and I surrendered to God. Now, as you know, I am totally into the faith. Nothing is more important to me than God and pleasing him. I am completely Catholic, I love the Church and all her teachings, about sex, about marriage, about contraception, but as I said, that was not always so.

"What I must tell you is that I have a venereal disease, herpes. It is controllable, but there are some dangers . . . [explain in detail the dangers]. So, I want you to know this now, before we go too far in this relationship, in case you may not want to deal with this."

She needs to be prepared for him to end the relationship when she tells him, although that may not always be necessary. Some diseases, such as AIDS, are so serious as to render marriage very unwise. Others, such as herpes, may be manageable and may not preclude marriage.

Abortion

What if a woman had an abortion? Even if it's been a long time, you have confessed it, and found peace in God's mercy, it will probably still affect your life a great deal. If you have nightmares about it, or if it still bothers you a good deal, then you should tell, because it will affect your relationship. Again, you have to make that decision yourself.

Homosexuality and Pedophilia

Past homosexual activity presents some challenges. If it was experimentation and not the result of a persisting same-sex attraction condition, I would say you need not mention it. If you have or have had a same-sex attraction or are bi-sexual, you should certainly mention this as soon as you enter courtship. Unless a person gets therapy and reduces considerably any same-sex attraction, he or she should not marry. This could be grounds for annulment, should a marriage take place.

And in today's world, the issue of pedophilia (sex with pre-adolescents) or ephebophilia (sex with adolescents) may arise. This must certainly be told to any prospective spouse early in courtship, since withholding it could be grounds for annulment. This may be one of the conditions which precludes marriage since there is no known psychological cure of pedophilia and such an attraction could be disastrous if a couple marries and has children.

Other Things From the Past

If a man has fathered a child, and the child is alive and well, even if adopted, he should reveal this from day one of a courtship, since the child may show up some day. The same goes for a woman who has given her child up for adoption.

Regarding past use of pornography, it would seem that this need not be mentioned, but an ongoing addiction to it should, since this could affect the relationship. Anyone who is addicted to pornography should attend Sexaholics Anonymous, or at least find a good spiritual guide to mentor them away from such activity.

Recent Sexual Sins

Now, some people may admit past sins, but they are recent. They may be, for example, just a month old. The first question to ask is, "Is this person converted?" The only logical answer is no, since a real conversion ordinarily takes several years. They may have the beginning of a conversion, but even they should not trust it until it has lasted a long time.

It's fair to ask how long it's been since a person has fallen into sins against chastity, but the question should be phrased diplomatically. It would be difficult and possibly embarrassing to ask, "How long has it been since your last sinful encounter?" It might be better to ask, "How long ago did you have a conversion on this?" If it's only been a short time, exercise caution. Some people have a way of converting when it's convenient, and reverting when it isn't. People, especially men, can be odd about chastity. They can be the sweetest, most dependable people in many different ways, but hopelessly committed to free sex. Sexual libertarians do not make good spouses.

The Mercy of God

While sin is a terrible thing, God's mercy far exceeds it. The Old Testament speaks abundantly of the mercy of God. For example Daniel 3:67 says, "Give thanks to the Lord for he is good, his *mercy* endures forever. . . ." One of Pope John Paul II's earliest encyclicals was *Dives in Misericordia*, literally "[God, who is] rich in Mercy" (Ephesians 2:4), about God's infinite mercy. The divine Mercy Chaplet, given to us through St. Maria Faustina, is aimed at helping us to realize the infinite mercy of God. God told her it was his greatest attribute.

Certainly we find in the lives of the saints, those such as Augustine and Mary Magdalene, wondrous examples of God's endless mercy. There is one saint, however, whose life seems to speak of this mercy more than that of any other: St. Margaret of Cortona.

Those who have many past sins and sometimes doubt the mercy of God for themselves will find her story inspiring.

Margaret was born in Laviano, Tuscany (present-day Italy) in 1247. Her mother died when Margaret was just seven. Her father remarried two years later but neither he nor his new wife provided the love Margaret needed. So she looked for love outside her home with the boys of her town. Her striking beauty, combined with her spirited nature, made her irresistibly attractive. She loved the attention, and gave in to their lustful desires. Before she was 17 the whole town knew of her sexual adventures. At 18 she ran off with a nobleman to live in his castle in the hills of Montepulciano. Though he promised to marry her, he never did, so she lived openly as his mistress for nine years.

It was only through tragedy that she reformed. When she was 27, her nobleman lover failed to return from a business trip. After days of searching, she was led by his dog to his murdered body, covered with leaves in the woods. She screamed and fainted. When she recovered she faced squarely the issue of her own death, her destiny. Where was her lover's soul now? Where would she end up for all eternity?

She left his castle and resolved to change her life. She ended up in Cortona, where she was given the grace of finding a kind priest to hear her confession. She began to pray unceasingly, and to live a life of deep penance, wearing rags for clothing, sleeping on the ground with a stone or piece of wood as a pillow, and seeking to humiliate herself in every way. When she asked God to remove her beauty, he refused. He told her he wanted to use it to have sinners come to her and be converted.

As time went on, she was able to draw closer and closer to the Lord through her prayer and penance. Once, when she had been pursuing holiness for many years, Our Lord said to her, "My daughter,

I will place you among the Seraphs, among the virgins whose hearts are flaming with the love of God."

"How can that be," she asked, "since I have spoiled myself with so many sins?"

"My daughter, your many penances have purified your soul from all the effects of sin to such a degree that your contrition and sufferings will reintegrate you into the purity of a virgin." For her love of chastity she would be "placed among the virgins."

Some time after, the Lord appeared with his angels and they gave her a white robe, a wedding ring and a crown. Then Jesus declared, "You are my spouse." This "mystical marriage," is said to be the highest spiritual state possible, in which the soul is constantly aware of God's presence and love.

After twenty-three years of prayer, penance and helping the sick and poor, Margaret died peacefully on February 22, 1297 at age 50. Almost immediately miracles began to occur at her grave, including the raising to life of twelve persons. Her body is incorrupt to this day, visible beneath the main altar of the Basilica of Cortona." She was canonized in 1728.

What an awesome, merciful God it is who can raise us from the depths of sin to the heights of holiness as he raised Margaret. Granted, once we seek and receive forgiveness, it is a hard road to make up for our sins, as Margaret discovered. But nothing is sweeter for the sinner than to travel that road back to a deep, peaceful intimacy with God, our ultimate spouse who will always take us back.

The Reformed Sinner

Do reformed sinners make good spouses? Some do, if they are truly reformed. One woman gave a talk on chastity some years back in our diocese. She commented that her greatest supporters in promoting chastity across the country were reformed sinners. After all, who was a greater promoter of Christianity than St. Paul, a converted persecutor of the Church?

If you are a reformed sinner and you are working at rebuilding your friendship with the Lord by prayer, frequent Mass attendance, and doing penance, don't mope about. Christ's blood washes clean! If you are alive in Christ, you can become a great marriage partner! God himself has invited you to be his spouse, and if you persevere you will be just that.

Summing It Up

It's probably a good idea to give your sweetheart a general idea of any past sins, especially if they might come up in your marriage, but spare the details. Giving details almost always causes problems. Be aware of the awesome mercy of God. If you're a reformed sinner, and you are trying to make up for your sins by prayer and penance, hold your head high. Christ did not die in vain!

Chapter Thirteen

Enjoying Singleness

One phenomenon I have noticed among single Catholics over the past ten or twenty years is that of the obsessive spouse-seeker. It may be the woman who frets that she is getting older, and if Mr. Right doesn't come along soon, she won't be able to have any children. Or it could be the man who laments the fact that he has not been able to find the right woman and he is miserable. In either case, they obsess over finding the right person. Some even marry someone who is quite dysfunctional, thinking such a relationship will be better than nothing.

The problem with all of this is that it betrays a serious lack of trust in God. God has a plan for us, and he's arranged things for our best interests, if we love him. St. Paul tells us in Romans 8:28, "We know that all things work for good for those who love God. . . ." Do we believe that? Do we believe it enough to say to God at whatever age you are, "Lord, I thank you for the fact that I am not married now. I praise you for that, because I know that this is something that will work for my good because I love you."

Methodist minister Merlin Carothers writes in *Prison to Praise* of the many miracles that occurred to him and others who had enough trust to praise God in all things, based on that quote from

Romans. Even when things seemed impossibly bad, these people praised God for the good he would bring from them, and indeed he did bring about good. How God loves trust!

God tells us over and over in Scripture that he is close to us and that we should trust him. "Blessed is the man who trusts in the Lord, whose hope is the Lord. He is like a tree planted by water, that sends out its roots by the stream, and does not fear when heat comes, for its leaves remain green, and is not anxious in the year of drought, for it does not cease to bear fruit" (Jeremiah 17: 7, 8).

And again in Matthew he says, "Look at the birds of the air: they neither sow nor reap nor gather into barns, and yet your heavenly Father feeds them. Are you not of more value than they? And which of you by being anxious can add one cubit to his span of life? . . . Therefore do not be anxious, saying, 'What shall we eat?' or 'What shall we drink?' or 'What shall we wear?' For the Gentiles seek all these things; and your heavenly Father knows that you need them all. But seek first his kingdom and his righteousness, and all these things shall be yours as well."

We might imagine Jesus saying to the single Christian, "Do not worry about when or whom you are to marry. Your heavenly Father knows you want a good, devout spouse. Seek first his Kingdom and his righteousness and this will be given you as well."

Perhaps the following quote is most apt for the concerned single Christian:

> Trust in the Lord, and do good; so you will dwell in the land, and enjoy security. Take delight in the Lord, and he will give you the desires of your heart. Commit your way to the Lord; trust in him, and he will act . . . Be still before the Lord, and wait patiently for him. (Psalm 37:3–5, 7)

Seek First His Kingdom

So how does all this translate into action? First, you must seek God's kingdom. How do you do that? Well, it begins with prayer. Real prayer. Prayer that takes some time. If you are really going to seek God's kingdom you must see it as Jesus tells us, as the pearl of great price: ". . . the kingdom of heaven is like a merchant in search of fine pearls, who, on finding one pearl of great value, went and sold all that he had and bought it" (Matthew 13: 46, 47). If this is really worth selling all you have to possess, your prayer should reflect that urgency.

As a young single person you are in a unique situation with regard to your time. You have more time than you will ever have until retirement. Don't waste this time moping around, feeling sorry for yourself because you haven't found a good spouse. This is the time to develop a strong prayer life.

Once you pray perhaps fifteen to thirty minutes a day, then look at the possibility of daily Mass. Can't do it? Schedule doesn't permit it? No problem. Ask the Lord to find a way for you. At one time I didn't think I had time either. I struggled to get up each morning for work. There was no way I would be able to get to 7 a.m. Mass each day, or so I thought. One day the Lord inspired me to try it and see if my health, which was never anything great, could survive. Not only did it survive, but it got better! I began going to daily Mass over 25 years ago and have been going ever since. It has been one of the greatest joys of my life. Many, many of our young, single Catholic men and women have started attending daily Mass, and it has been a great source of blessings in their lives. So, just open your heart a little bit to the possibility of daily Mass now, while you are single. Ask the Lord to show you a way that you can do it. You might find he'll surprise you.

Read the Saints

One of the things you can do to keep your religious motivation high is to read the lives and writings of the saints. This is extremely important if you wish to make progress spiritually. Do it now, while you are single, and you will stir your heart to a strong spiritual life. And rather than being obsessed with finding a spouse, you will be focused on your salvation and your growth toward that goal.

Get Support in the Faith

Reading about the saints will help keep you motivated to live the faith, but so will having good friends who share your faith. So many young single Catholics feel alone because they are trying to live their faith in a pagan world, without any peer support. If you want to have a real Christian courtship, you must make every effort to move in good, Christian circles. You should surround yourself with people who believe as you do. It's not enough to look for Mr. or Miss Right at solidly Catholic events. You must make friends with Catholics and develop a "family" of Catholic peers, people you can get together with and live a real Christian social life.

In the early nineties we started two groups in the Washington, DC area, one for men called the St. Lawrence Society and one for women called the St. Catherine Society. They were created to help men and women provide mutual support in living the Faith.

The St. Catherine Society, named after St. Catherine of Alexandria, the patron of single women, began in 1992, and almost from the start the women realized that they could be openly Catholic, and not worry about what others would think. "Father, it's such a joy coming to this group. I feel so . . . safe here. It's really OK to be a Catholic for a few hours." She was bright, energetic, and really working at her faith. Some time later she was having coffee with an old boyfriend and he asked her if she still practiced the faith.

"Sure," she replied.

"You go to Mass every Sunday?" he asked.

"Well, actually, I go every day."

"No sex?" he continued.

"No sex."

He was not ready to sign on to her program, but he was impressed. She was an attractive, successful woman, fully in tune with the world, and alive in her love for God. And she is not the only one living this way. More than 60 percent of the women in the group pray the Rosary and attend Mass daily, and read spiritual books. And when they have a party, everyone wants to come, because they are fun to be with.

The St. Lawrence Society, named after St. Lawrence, the patron of single men, is equally vibrant. More than half the members go to Mass and pray daily, and almost all of them want to grow in their faith. A new St. Lawrence member recently commented about the two groups, "I've never seen anything like this in any city. You have something beautiful here. Don't ever take it for granted."

Both the St. Catherine Society and the St. Lawrence Society are for young, single Catholics who take their faith seriously, but don't take themselves too seriously. They are successful, and alive and growing in their faith.

The single-sex format works, I believe, because women and men are willing to be part of a singles group in which they have social opportunities, but in which they also have the opportunity to cultivate their faith with others of the same sex, without having to deal with dating issues all the time. In both groups a strong social element is present, but spirituality has always been primary. This and the single-sex approach are the things that have kept the groups from becoming lonely hearts clubs.

The meetings involve prayer — usually the Rosary — followed by discussion of the faith, and dinner. A list of members is passed out at the meetings so they can contact each other between the monthly meetings, for lunch or whatever, and develop real friendships. The members have felt free to speak about how much they have gained from daily Mass or praying the daily Rosary. A number were quite surprised to find chaste courtships well within their reach and would discuss this freely with the others. And some have shared their joy at spending time before the Blessed Sacrament. All of this has had the effect of encouraging others to do likewise.

For several years each group has rented a house at the beach for a week, usually a block apart. I have often joined them for the week, saying Mass each day. I'll never forget the Saturday night when everyone went out after dinner to the beach at about 9 p.m., sat in a circle, and prayed the Rosary together. One time at the beach when I returned from my holy hour, one of the women asked me if she could join me. I said "Sure." It occurred to me to invite *all* the 15 women and eight men if they would like to go. The next morning about 10 people showed up at church to pray a holy hour!

Each group has its yearly traditions: the men host a picnic in May each year in honor of the pope, and the women have their Christmas party, on or near Epiphany. They also have other small social gatherings during the year. The goal from the beginning was to establish a new Christian culture, a kind of family for young, single Catholics. For many, it has worked. One of the nicest things for me to see is the life-long friendships they have formed. Long after they marry, many are still in touch with each other and getting together. Faith is a great source of bonding.

I would hope that many single Catholics reading this book would consider forming such groups in their own area. It will help you to make good use of your single years to grow in the faith, and it will make those years far more pleasant. If there are not enough young people around to do that, at least try to meet a handful of young men and women who share your faith, and socialize with them. You'll be pleasing God and improving your social life at the same time.

Nail Down Job Goals

While you are single is a good time to figure out what your job goals are and work in that direction. If you are unhappy with your work, now is the time to perhaps take a vocational test or at least look around to see if you might enjoy something else better. If you are happy with your profession, now is the time to get the education or skills you will need to stay in that profession. In any case, the time to solidify your professional life is now, not after you start courtship, or worse yet, after you marry.

Learn to Live Simply

One of the greatest sources of marital problems is money. The time to get responsible about money is now, not when you get married. The time to start saving for a house — or even buying a house as an investment — is now. Many young people are terribly extravagant with their money when they are single, and then when they do marry they wish they had been a bit more sensible. They wish they had lived more simply.

Janet Luhrs makes an excellent point in her book, *The Simple Living Guide*:

Simple living is about living deliberately. You *choose* your existence rather than go through life on automatic pilot. . . . You could have any level of income, but you hang on to a good chunk of your income, whatever it is. Simple living is about having money in the bank and a zero balance on your credit card statement. . . .

Living deeply means living intimately . . . closely tied to the people, places, and things in your life. When you simplify, you'll have space and time to know and love people in a deeper way. . . . You'll surround yourself with people who like and love you for who you are deep inside, rather than the professional or other type of persona you project to the world.

Spending moderately, investing wisely, living simply, being generous with the poor and the Church, all these things are part of Christian living. They are not optional for the Christian. Now is the time to start applying your faith to your pocketbook. You'll be preparing well not only for marriage, but for the Kingdom as well.

And living simply is not only about money. It's about time as well. Janet Luhrs describes the omnipresent "time famine":

Our time famine is really an intimacy famine. It is much easier to stay busy and frantic than it is to love and know ourselves and others deeply.

We can't take the time to be sensitive to others and truly care for them when we are in a constant hurry. Relationships take time to nurture.

Intimacy and relationships are the things that will fulfill us as persons. They are the things that bring us real happiness. Sometimes single people are so hyperactive that they can't sit still long enough to relate to others in a significant way. One man came to the beach with us, but we hardly ever saw him. He was here and there, out jogging, buying something, or driving off sixty miles away to have a date. He couldn't sit still! Many, many people — single and married — need to slow down and take time to "smell the roses" of good, quiet friendships. How important this is for psychological and spiritual health!

Schedule just a few things in a day. Lean towards under-scheduling rather than over-scheduling. Relax. Enjoy quiet evenings in long conversation. Life will be much sweeter and so will courtship.

Cut Out Most TV

When I was a young engineer, I would come home from work or from working out, and would turn on the TV while I cooked and ate dinner. Then, when I was finished dinner, I just kept on watching into the night. The whole night was wasted. Later, I realized my foolishness, and began to eat in the dining room while reading a magazine or book. That was a great step forward. All of a sudden I had much more time to live my life and be with friends. And, of course, I wasn't being dragged down by the morally-challenged TV mentality.

So, if you want to have a devout, productive life, turn the television off, except when there is something really good on. Pick your programs carefully. Use the time for reading or being with friends.

Summing It Up

When you are single is not the time to longingly and anxiously look forward to marriage, but the time to develop into a better person. Work hard on your relationship with God by prayer, daily Mass if possible, and receiving the sacraments. Get support in your faith by reading about the saints, and forming groups or at least friendships with other real Catholics to make living the faith easier. Decide what your professional goals are and take the necessary first steps to achieve those goals. Strive to live simply with regard to both time and money, so as to be free to develop good, enriching friendships. Cut television watching way back. If you do these things while you are single, you'll be ready when the right person comes along, and more importantly, you'll please God.

Chapter Fourteen

Christian Marriage — Part One

Love: The Form of Marriage

Some of the topics covered in the next two chapters on marriage may seem a bit premature, since our topic is courtship, not marriage. However, it is important to think about them now, before you marry. Then when you get married, you'll have an idea of what you'll have to deal with, and you'll be ready. Many wrong decisions have been made because couples had no clue about what was coming, and when they had to decide, they just went along with "the world." The further the world gets from God, the more mistakes it makes, especially regarding marriage. Indeed, the purpose of courtship is to discover and build a relationship for marriage. If you are going to have a Christian Courtship, it is a good idea to reflect for a moment on what a good, Christian Marriage is like.

First, what is marriage *for*? It's rather a profound question when you think about it, one which the fathers of the Second Vatican Council pondered for a long time. The Council taught "By their inner nature, the very institution of marriage and conjugal love, are ordained to the procreation and education of children and it is in them that they are crowned as by their summit."[1] Further on it added, ". . . A man and a woman, who by their covenant of conjugal love 'are no longer two, but one flesh' (Matthew 19:6), give mutual help and service to each other through an intimate union of their persons and actions. . . ." It also taught that spouses in marriage, by fulfilling their conjugal and parental mission, "further more and more their own perfection and mutual sanctification, and thus together they give glory to God."

How might we put this more simply? *Marriage is an institution in which a couple commits to serve each other in love for life, to grow in holiness and raise saints for God.*

The Sacrament — Commitment

Why is the divorce rate in the United States about 50 percent for all marriages and close to 75 percent for those who live together before marriage?[2] Perhaps one reason is that many seem unaware of what a large undertaking marriage is. Marriage vows are a big responsibility.

Once a woman came to see me about her husband who had left a year or so earlier. He wanted to come back, but she was very hurt by his running off. He had said some terrible things to her and some even worse things to her parents. She wanted to know what she could do about an annulment. "How could I ever take him back?" she asked.

I got out the Bible and began to read to her from Genesis: ". . . a man leaves his father and mother and clings to his wife, and the two of them become one body" (Genesis 2:24).

"You made a vow didn't you?" I asked her.

"Yes."

"Before God?"

"Yes," she answered.

"Then don't you think you should do everything in your power to keep that vow?"

"I guess so. But, what about my parents? How can I accept what he did to them?" she asked.

"A man leaves father and mother and clings to his spouse." I replied.

"You mean I must be more devoted to my spouse than my parents?"

"That's it," I said. "A married person should never let a member of their family, even one's own mother, come between her and her husband, other than perhaps to save one's life. One should never think he or she must be more faithful to parents or any family member than his own spouse. Marriage creates a sacred bond which far transcends every family tie." She took him back. They've been through more difficulties, but they are still together.

It amazes me how often people forget what they promised on their wedding day. That woman would have been delighted if I had told her she could get an annulment, and she might have sought one.

This is not what God intended. Jesus spoke about marriage as follows: "What . . . God has joined together, let not man put asunder" (Matthew 19:6). He also said in Luke 16:18, "Every one who divorces his wife and marries another commits adultery, and he who marries a woman divorced from her husband commits adultery."

How quickly we forget what the marriage vows are. They are a commitment before God to serve each other in love until death, to be a sign, a sacrament, to the world of the covenantal love between Christ and his Church, between God and his people. But when things get rough, how quickly Christians sound like the rest of the world.

There is something we should realize about any commitment: It is not only a curtailment of freedom, but a manifestation of freedom as well. If you never commit to anything, your freedom is worthless. *Tout choix est un sacrifice* (Every choice is a sacrifice) as the French say. But if we never choose, what good is our freedom? To choose, to commit, and to stay committed is the noblest exercise of freedom.

Every commitment to a person, every friendship and every love, brings bonds. Loving God means doing many things we'd rather not do and avoiding some things we'd like to do. You cannot be in relation to another without some limitations on your behavior. And, being in relationships, with God, with spouse, with others, is the only thing that will fulfill us as persons. Not success, not wealth, not fame, not pleasure. Only good relationships will make us happy.

Think about these vows you and your spouse will make when you marry. "I, John, take you, Mary, to be my wife. I promise to be true to you in good times and in bad, in sickness and in health. I will love you and honor you all the days of my life."

What an awesome promise! Think about that long and hard if you intend to marry.

I will be true to you in good times and bad. That means I will be faithful to you when things are not going well between us. I will be faithful to you when there's no money, when you come home late, when we both are miserably unhappy. I will be there for you when you gain weight, when you turn gray, when you become bald, when your beauty fades. Marriage is not about maximizing pleasure, but about following a call from God to love this person selflessly and to raise up saints together. It's not about drawing all the joy and delight you can from your emotional love together, but about building a serene, quiet, enduring friendship through kindness, graciousness, and generous self-giving, even when it hurts; and spending yourselves together nurturing godly children. And, of course, through this, helping each other to grow in holiness.

I will be true to you in sickness and in health. That means I will be faithful to you even if you get MS, or some other serious disease and are bed-ridden. I will be there when you get old, when you use a walker, when you are in a wheelchair. I will be there for you.

I will love you and honor you all the days of my life. In other words, I will work for your good, your happiness every day, no matter what happens, no matter how unkind you were to me last night, no matter how hurt I feel. I will always work for your good. And not only will I love you, I will *honor* you as well. That means I will respect you; I will uphold your dignity. I will not treat you lightly or as an inferior. I will hold you up as someone special, someone precious to me. And, I'll do this every day of my life.

This is the vow you make before God, before his altar. In other words, it would be one thing to promise this to your spouse, but a vow calls on God as witness, so that if you fail to keep a vow, it's far more serious than just breaking a promise or a contract. You are giving your word to your spouse before God.

Meditate on this long and hard before you agree to it. Are you really ready to make this sort of commitment? Do you have the grace to keep this sort of vow? The character? Meditate on this every day for months before your marriage. If you are not willing to use every ounce of your moral and psychological and physical strength to fulfill this vow, don't make it. You may not be able to be sure you're marrying the right person, but you can be absolutely sure of your willingness to work at your marriage. This is a major religious undertaking. Do not take it lightly.

Your marriage commitment is not just about you and your spouse. It is to be a sign to the world of the love between Christ and his

Church (Ephesians 5:32). Would Christ ever leave the Church? Never! He said he would be with us always, until the end of time (Matthew 28:20) and he will. You and your spouse are a symbol to the world of that covenental love. Are you ready for that? Are you willing to work harder at this relationship than anything else you have ever done in your life? Are you willing to swallow your pride a hundred times a year to build a loving peace in your home? Are you willing to say "I love you" to someone who has said mean and nasty things to you, even to someone who has acted like your worst enemy lately? Are you willing to do this, because you promised, you *vowed*, to love him/her?

Think of the immensity of this vow when you consider marrying after only a nine-month courtship. Think of the immensity of this vow when you might want to marry at 21 or 22. Think of the immensity of this vow when many among friends and family tell you this person is trouble. Think of the immensity of this vow when you want to marry one who has no faith, no use for God. Pray about your marriage. Pray for the grace to make the vow with a deep awareness of what you are doing, and to keep that vow until death. And, pray that the one you marry will do the same, for this is what it means to enter into the *sacrament* of holy matrimony.

Honor Your Spouse

When you marry, you also promise to *honor* your spouse. That means you will always respect him/her. You will always uphold his/her dignity as a human person. You will do this, not because he/she deserves it, but because you vowed to do it at God's altar.

How do you do this? You resolve now, long before your wedding, to always be polite to your spouse, to try to say "please" and "thank you" consistently, or ". . . if you would be so kind."

Some people think this all sounds too formal and difficult to remember. Formal or not, the couples who do this are extremely successful in their marriages. And, as for remembering, once you make it a habit, you don't have to think about it any more. It takes several weeks, perhaps even months to make it a habit, but once you do, you'll have a marital treasure. Hang on to it for dear life. It will work wonders in your marriage.

Also, develop nice names for each other. One friend of mine calls his wife his "bride" even though they've been married over forty years. Names like "sweetheart" or "love of my life" or "darling," or even "honey-bun" (not without a pinch of facetiousness) can warm the heart of a spouse even after thirty or forty or fifty years of marriage.

This is all part of honoring your spouse. When you marry, do it every day. Remember, you promised.

Communicating Dissatisfaction Diplomatically

Another element of honoring your spouse is to let him or her know you are unhappy with certain behavior, without destroying him or her. This is vital. Three short rules go far in keeping harmony in a relationship:

1. Try to be humorous. You may be hopping mad at some rude way your husband asked you to do something. Instead of coming back with, "How dare you speak to me that way!" which has a good chance of starting World War III, try something like, "Now Mr. Jones, do ya suppose you could put that a bit more politely?"

2. Think before speaking. And your thought should be something along the line of "Now how would Jesus or Mary act in this situation?"

3. Choose the right time. Let's say your spouse said something quite inappropriate to your child. It's best not to lambaste him or her right there. Later, when you're alone together, say something like, "Honey, could we talk about that little incident this morning?" Or, what if your husband proposes some lame-brained investment scheme? Rather than telling him what you think — that it sounds idiotic — be wise. Say, "Well, let's give that some thought, dear." Hopefully, when *he* thinks about it some more, he'll see the folly of it. Even if he doesn't, you'll have time to think of a way to kindly tell him you think it's a crazy idea. Remember, one of the elements of honoring someone is to try to build them up, not tear them down.

Fidelity

Now is the time to think about how you are going to protect your fidelity in marriage. Some might be thinking "Well, that won't be a problem. I will be faithful, period." Would that everyone who ever said that lived it. Marriage is a long-term proposition, and couples can go through some long, drawn-out periods of bad communications, bad tempers, bad blood. This is when infidelity can become a real temptation.

There are two types of infidelity: physical and spiritual. The physical we call adultery. The spiritual we call "spiritual adultery" and it can be just as harmful as the other. The latter involves no sex, but instead entails having most of your emotional needs met by another person outside your marriage.

So often spouses seem to unwittingly slide into infidelity, of either type, without even knowing how it happens. It usually occurs when things are not going well at home, although not always. You ride to a meeting with someone, or you go out to lunch with a co-worker and the heart begins to stir. All of a sudden you find this other person so much more understanding, so much more considerate of your needs than your spouse. (Of course, if you were to leave your spouse and marry this one, in ten years someone else would be "so much more understanding, etc.")

So how do you avoid this mess? First, you work very hard to make sure things go well at home. You study good books on communication. If there are real problems, you visit your priest to help you to see ways to heal your relationship with your spouse, and if necessary you get professional counseling.

But, even if things are going fine at home, you can still get into trouble. An important principle to remember is never to unnecessarily be alone with a member of the opposite sex for any long period of time or successive periods of time. One woman told me she loved her husband but that she had fallen in love with her boss at work. She was confused by this. I asked her if she went out to lunch with him from time to time. She said yes. I said, "Try never to be alone with him, and try not to think about him. This feeling will pass in just a few months." Every married person should avoid being alone unnecessarily with a member of the opposite sex for long periods.

Some people are very naive when it comes to this. They think such caution is totally unnecessary. Or they are too prideful. They think, "Well, I'm secure in my marriage. I don't need to take such precautions." One of the most important adages is "There but for the grace of God go you or I." Anyone who thinks himself above taking certain precautions is at most risk for getting into trouble. It is amazing what behavior we slide into when we think ourselves impervious to it.

What a Husband Can Do for His Wife

There are certain things that a husband is uniquely qualified to do for his wife. The first is to let her know that he loves her. What is the most effective way to do this? First, by often telling her "I love you," whether you feel like it or not. And then, by always treating her heart with the utmost respect and tenderness. This is better than sending roses, better than buying her beautiful jewelry or a new car or building her a house in the mountains, although all of these are nice, too. But most women tell me they aren't necessary. What they want is caring and compassion when they are feeling blue, for whatever reason. Just hold her when things aren't right, and simply tell her how important her happiness is to you.

If she's upset with you, *don't try to defend yourself!* Just rush to her side and tell her you're sorry you have hurt her, whether you were right or wrong in what you did. Later you can sort out how to deal with this situation next time. When things have calmed down (by at least a day or two) you can always ask, "Sweetheart, I need your advice on how to handle such a situation in the future without upsetting you."

Christian Sex

Another priceless thing a husband can do is to adapt to the physical timing of his wife in sexual relations. Vatican II taught about conjugal love as follows:

This love is uniquely expressed and perfected through the act proper to marriage. Hence, the actions within marriage by which the couple are united intimately and chastely are noble and worthy. Expressed in a manner which is truly human, these actions signify and foster the mutual self-donation by which spouses enrich each other with a joyful and a ready mind.

By saying the marriage act "expresses" and "perfects" conjugal love, the Council was saying that this act celebrates the existence of this love, proclaims it, and by perfecting it, forms the future of this love. As such, the act should be carried out in a way that is truly loving. A way that is primarily aimed at pleasing the *other*, not the self. In this way it will help the love between husband and wife to grow. It will not only be a *fruit* of making the lifelong commitment of marriage, but a way of fostering and nourishing that love.

The marital act should not primarily be about receiving, but giving. It is about accommodating oneself to the other's needs. To determine the sort of accommodation necessary, we need to ask, which one is more likely to experience the pleasure of marital intercourse, the man or the woman? Clearly the man. Often the man will reach orgasm before his wife, and in fact, she may not reach a climax at all in a given act, especially if the man is unaware of what is happening in his wife.

Thus, the man has the greater job of accommodation. In fact, this should be clear when St. Paul speaks of the husband as the head of the wife: headship in the Christian context primarily means service. The husband must be the initiator of love and serve his wife.

How does he serve her in marital relations? By accommodating himself to her tempo. A woman is slow to get aroused and thus requires patient stimulation by her husband. He should use a great deal of self-control to delay completion of the act until he is sure she is sufficiently ready. Only then should he complete the act. After this, she is slow to come down, and so he must attend to her affectionately as she gently descends from the mountain of a sexual high, and not simply roll over and go to sleep. Men who have accommodated their wives in this way have brought upon themselves untold blessings.

The goal for a man in learning loving accommodation and practicing it should be to fulfill his marriage vow: to love and honor his wife. He should rejoice in making her happy in this act of intimacy. Men should know from the start that this is not easy. It takes real self-control.

Even Catholic moral theology acknowledges this difference in tempo, by allowing the man to stimulate his wife right after he reaches a climax, to insure that she might also.[3] Of course, this should not be necessary if the man accommodates his wife adequately. This is all part of the respect a man should have for his wife.

Pius XII in an address to midwives in October 1951 had a great insight regarding respect for today's married couples:

> There are some who would allege that happiness in marriage is in direct proportion to the reciprocal enjoyment in conjugal relations. It is not so: indeed, happiness in marriage is in direct proportion to the mutual respect of the partners, even in their intimate relations. . . .

One more thing. As one bride-to-be put it, "I want to be made love to verbally before I make love physically." In other words, it is a very smart thing, indeed a very loving thing, for a husband to spend some time speaking about intimate things with his wife for a time, before having relations. The best sex is not the most passionate, but the most personal.

Even in the marital bedroom, love requires a dying to self, especially for the man who by his leadership is to be the initiator of love. If he dies in this way, he will live in a newness of life with his grateful wife.

Bedroom Limitations?

Are there moral limits as to what husband and wife can do in terms of sexual intimacy? Yes, indeed. While all dignified types of foreplay are allowed, the encounter must always end in natural intercourse with the penis in the vagina. Although oral-genital contact stimulation is not prohibited as foreplay if mutually agreed upon,[4] my own opinion is that this should be avoided except to remedy male erectile difficulties.[5] In fact, from what I have seen in marriages, it would be better if it were avoided completely. Why? Because this sort of activity is impersonal, and sexual encounters should be personal to maintain human dignity. And, of course, if this activity is repugnant to either party, it would be wrong for the other to seek it. I think it is safe to say that anal-genital contact is not licit, since it is impersonal, and is hazardous to one's health. Also, it hardly seems in keeping with human dignity. In any case, couples should never allow pleasure to become the main goal of sexual intercourse, as is often the case when one or both seek various sorts of "creative" foreplay.

In that same talk to midwives, Pope Pius XII warned against becoming slaves of sensuality in marriage when he wrote, "the gravity and sanctity of the Christian moral law do not admit an unchecked satisfaction of the sexual instinct tending only to pleasure and enjoyment."

However, there is no harm in seeking pleasure in the conjugal act as a secondary goal:

> Husband and wife, therefore, by seeking and enjoying this pleasure do no wrong whatever. They accept what the Creator has destined for them. Nevertheless, here also, husband and wife must know how to keep themselves within the limits of a just moderation. As with the pleasure of food and drink so with the sexual they must not abandon themselves without restraint to the impulses of the senses.

One other thought regarding limits. When a couple does anything which inevitably arouses either one (usually the man gets aroused first), they should plan on having sex. A couple came to see me once because the husband was very upset. She had invited him to join her in the shower one morning, and when he wanted to have sex, she wasn't interested. He was right to be angry. If a wife invites her husband to shower with her, she needs to realize that morally, it's a package deal. It's not right to get him all stirred up in the shower and then prance off. If she turns him on, she needs to follow through and have relations. To put it a different way, if a woman doesn't want to have sex with her husband, she has a moral obligation not to intentionally get him aroused (and vice versa).

Provide Her Some Zip

Another way a man can adapt to his wife is to be acutely aware of her needs as a woman. Most men can be happy going to work every day 9 to 5, eating three meals a day, and watching a ball game on Sunday. Not so, women. They like some variety in their lives. The man who knows this and tries to provide it will be way ahead of the game.

I encourage women to provide some of their own fun each week, such as playing tennis or going out with the girls. A woman should not be dependent on her husband for *all* her fun. Otherwise she becomes too dependent, and may start to nag him.

Nonetheless, the husband can play an important role in helping his wife meet her need for a little color in her life. He should ask her on a date every week or two. (Just as in courtship, he should call her by Tuesday for the weekend, and have the evening all planned. If he really wants to warm her heart, he could arrange for the baby-sitter himself.) Once in a while he should take her away for a weekend, too.

What Every Wife Can Do

What can the wife do to make her husband happy? The first thing, it seems, is to provide a warm, happy, attractive home. Whenever he comes home, a wife should greet him with a smile and a hug, and make him feel comfortable, even if she's mad at him. This is his cave, and it's important his entry there is pleasant. She can bring up unpleasant topics later, but not when he first comes in.

Some of the women in our couple's group greet their husbands warmly when they come home, and after the children greet him, they send the children off for half an hour, and just let Dad stare into space if he wants, to simply wind down. After that, he's on for the evening. Something else along that line: sometimes a man just doesn't want to talk, especially when he is tired. A good wife will be sensitive to this, and wait for more opportune times to bring things up.

Another thing which delights many a husband is for the wife to cook him something special. She should always try to make his dinner experience a pleasant one, cooking with the spices he likes, and always adding some extra little touches which show him she cares.

To be sure, it is very important for a wife to be receptive to marital relations when he is interested, and should not refuse him without a serious reason. However, this doesn't mean she can't coach him to realize the importance of sharing intimate thoughts and tender, gentle affection during the day to put her in the mood for having intercourse. She should diplomatically make it clear that while she likes to share marital intimacy with him, if he is sensitive to her emotional and physical needs, she will be far more receptive to his desires. Relations out of love will always be far more delightful than relations out of duty.

One other thing that a woman can do for her husband is to take care of herself. By that, I mean it is important for her to get her rest, proper nourishment, and exercise. She should also get out and have some good, clean fun at least once a week. Whether it's a sport like tennis or golf, or sewing lessons, or book discussion clubs, a woman should have some enjoyable time planned into her schedule.

What Both Can Do

Here is something you both should do. Hang a crucifix, where you will see it often, and remind yourselves everyday, "Love involves a cross. It's not for wimps!" Another thing is to go out with other good Catholic couples from time to time, or invite others to your house. One thing the couples in my parish do is to get together for our monthly "Cana Clubs" in which seven or eight couples meet for dinner, prayer, and discussion of the faith. Finally, try not to criticize. Try to give at least two compliments for every criticism.

Pray Together

It's essential for couples, and when the children come along, for families to pray together every night. Make this a real priority when you marry. It is the best insurance against divorce. According to figures quoted in *Soul* magazine in March-April 1990, the divorce rate for couples praying the Rosary together every day is one in 500, as compared to the national average of one in two.

How Do You Know if You Need Counseling?

If and when things get really bad in Christian marriage, the solution is counseling, not divorce. So how does a couple know if they need counseling? Here are some telltale signs:

1. One or both go through a week or more refusing to talk to the other.
2. One or both has gotten entangled with someone else even if no adultery is involved. (It could be "spiritual adultery.")
3. Due to difficulties in the relationship the couple hasn't had marital relations for over a month.
4. There is a lot of anger between the two whenever they argue.

For couples in this sort of difficulty, counseling is a no-brainer. They have nothing to lose, everything to gain. In this age, when so many are getting married in their 30's and later, and so many come from dysfunctional situations, it just isn't reasonable to think that one will never need counseling. It takes humility to do it, but it is far less humbling than divorce.

If the couple know a wise and holy priest, they should start with him. If the problem is not something complicated, often he can help them solve it in one or two meetings. And, of course, he's free. Free counseling is nothing to sneeze at. Furthermore, it may be easier to go to a priest who one or both may already know. If he can't help, or if they don't know a satisfactory priest, then they might get a referral from a friend who has had good results. In any case, they should go to someone who believes in God and believes in the permanence of marriage.

Moral theologian Germain Grisez writes in *The Way of The Lord Jesus, Volume II: Living A Christian Life,* "Couples who see the need for [marital] help have a grave obligation to make any sacrifices necessary to obtain it; they should not delay in the vain hope that the trouble will go away with the mere passage of time."

Regardless of whom they go to, if he or she is of no help after two sessions, they should stop and go to someone else. No one should waste their time on someone who is incompetent.

Summing It Up

When you marry, make your commitment to your spouse a strong one. By God's grace make it an iron-clad promise to God and your wife or husband. Honor your spouse, especially by being polite in every situation. When you're not happy with your spouse, and it's worth mentioning, tell him or her, *gently*. Take no chances with fidelity. Don't unnecessarily spend time alone with members of the opposite sex.

Men, when you marry, always treat the heart of your wife with great care. Adapt your lovemaking to her tempo, and talk to her about important things before having relations. Provide your wife some zip.

Women, look forward to providing a happy, attractive "cave" for your husband. Greet him warmly whenever he comes in. Know when not to talk. Cook with love and coach him on how to prepare you for marital relations. Take care of yourself and have some fun weekly!

Never let in-laws come between you. Pray together every evening. And, promise each other, long before the wedding, that you will get counseling if real problems arise in the marriage.

Endnotes

1. *Gaudium et Spes*, Second Vatican Council, n. 48. (Translation from the Latin here, and subsequently, is my own unless otherwise indicated.)

2. David Popenoe and Barbara Dafoe Whitehead, social scientists at Rutgers University, cite a 1992 study that cohabiting couples have a 46 percent higher probability of divorce than non-cohabitors ("Should We Live Together?" at http://marriage.rutgers.edu). Some suggest that those willing to cohabitate are less conventional and less committed to marriage. Of course! The Church is not suggesting that people maintain their worldly views and stop cohabiting. We're encouraging people to develop real Christian attitudes toward sex and marriage, thereby avoiding cohabitation and a divorce rate of about 74 percent.

3. See, for example, Germain Grisez, *The Way of The Lord Jesus, Volume II: Living A Christian Life*, Quincy, IL: Franciscan Press, 1993, p. 642. Grisez acknowledges that either the husband or the wife may perform this stimulation. See also John R. Cavanagh, *Fundamental Marriage Counseling*, Milwaukee: Bruce Publishing Co., 1962, p. 170. Vice versa is not permitted because there should be no need for it after he reaches a climax.

4. See Germain Grisez, *The Way of The Lord Jesus, Volume II: Living A Christian Life*, p. 641. Grisez also allows for manual stimulation or self-stimulation as foreplay. Also see Ronald Lawler, OFM Cap., Joseph Boyle, Jr., and William E. May, *Catholic Sexual Ethics*, Huntington, IN: Our Sunday Visitor, 1985, pp. 172, 173. I mention this delicate subject (indeed, shocking to some) here because it comes up more often nowadays, in the wake of certain presidential revelations. It seems about half the people do not know of this allowance, and the other half know about it and tend to impose it unjustly on the other, or to use it indiscriminately. I firmly believe it should never be used merely as a way to expand the horizon of pleasure, or out of curiosity, but only as a remedy for the rare case of a man having difficulty preparing for marital intercourse.

5. Germain Grisez, *The Way of The Lord Jesus, Volume III: Difficult Moral Questions*, Quincy, IL: Franciscan Press, 1997, pp. 133 and 136. Grisez speaks of the moral liceity of this sort of contact in a situation where the man can only achieve an erection by such activity.

Chapter Fifteen

Christian Marriage — Part Two

༄

Children: The Fruit of Marriage

The fact that marriage and its form, conjugal love, are ordered to having and nurturing children is found in the very word matrimony. This contains two Latin words, *matri*, meaning mother, and *munus*, meaning mission. So, marriage is the mission of motherhood (and fatherhood). Marriage is about a husband and wife loving each other so much that their love overflows into bringing forth children, who are its greatest crown.

Vatican II spoke glowingly about the blessing of children: "Children are really the supreme gift of marriage and contribute very much to the good of their parents."

Additionally, "As living members of the family, children contribute in their own way to the sanctification of their parents. For they will respond to the benefits given by their parents with sentiments of gratitude, with love and trust. They will help them as children customarily do, in hard times and in the loneliness of their old age." And, finally,

Thus, trusting in divine Providence and cultivating the spirit of sacrifice, Christian spouses glorify the Creator and strive toward perfection in Christ, when with generous human and Christian responsibility they carry out the duty to procreate. Among spouses who fulfill in this way their God-given mission, particular mention should be made of those who, after wise and common deliberation, generously undertake to bring up suitably even a relatively large number of children.

So, children contribute to the good, and indeed, the sanctification of their parents. They show their parents gratitude, love and trust for their kindness. They help their parents in their old age. Parents, by fulfilling their mission of having children, glorify God and grow in perfection; and thus, parents who generously bring forth and educate a large number of children are to be given recognition.[1]

Pope John Paul II also spoke of the precious gift of children in *Familiaris consortio*:

In its most profound reality, love is essentially a gift; and conjugal love, while leading the spouses to the reciprocal "knowledge" which makes them "one flesh," does not end with the couple, because it makes them capable of the greatest possible gift, the gift by which they become cooperators with God for giving life to a new human person. Thus the couple, while giving themselves to one another, give not just themselves but also the reality of children, who are a living reflection of their love, a permanent sign of conjugal unity and a living and inseparable synthesis of their being a father and a mother.

We might add to the above list of benefits for parents in having children the fact that children, in their early helplessness, draw parents out and beyond themselves to love them, and to achieve their fulfillment as parents and educators. Children are often new and special friends for the parents. Children, by their very existence, give witness to the love between husband and wife for all eternity. Children are a source of deepening spousal friendship since they are a common interest which draws husband and wife together. Children often form a link between the parents and the community, thereby opening new horizons for friendships.

So, as you think about bringing forth children for God in your marriage, think not so much about what they will cost you, but how they will enrich you, the blessings they will bring. And, in keeping with reason, try for lots of these blessings.

Population Explosion?

"But Father," you may ask, "what about the population explosion?" Many years ago, Julian Simon,[2] Professor of Business Administration at the University of Maryland, began to research this so-called "population explosion" problem.

> Ironically, when I started to work on population studies, I assumed that the accepted view was sound. I aimed to help the world contain its "exploding" population. . . . But my reading and research led me into confusion. Though the then standard economic theory of population . . . asserted that a higher population growth implies a lower standard of living, the available empirical data did not support that theory. My technical 1977 book . . . arrived at a theory implying that

population growth has positive economic effects in the long run, although there are costs in the short run.[3]

His conclusion in his voluminous book *The Ultimate Resource II* is that a population which slowly increases is best for economic growth. He claims that reducing population growth is not the way to increase affluence, but vice versa. Helping countries to develop and have more affluence is the way to reduce excessive population growth.[4]

In 1999 business consultant Peter Drucker wrote, "the most important single new certainty — if only because there is no precedent for it in all of history — is the collapsing birthrate in the developed world."[5] At the turn of the 21st century, the birthrate in western Europe was well below replacement level of 2.1 children per fertile couple. The birthrate in the United States was just under two, still under the replacement level. Thus, if there is a population problem in the developed world, it's not one of *over*-population.

'We're Going to Wait a While'

Years ago I was preparing a couple for marriage. She was 34 and he was 36. The wife-to-be told me they were going to wait awhile before starting a family

"Are you serious?" I asked. "You're 34 years old. You may not be able to have children if you wait."

"We're only going to wait a few months."

"Why do you want to wait?" I asked.

"Well, we want to get settled for a while first," she replied.

"But marriage is 'ordained to the procreation and education of children,' as Vatican II put it. Look, God knows how much time you need to get settled. You should be spontaneous in your lovemaking when you first marry, especially on your honeymoon. Why not let God help you with this?" I asked her.

"You mean we should give control to God here?"

"Sure. You're only going to have so many chances to have children at your age. You want to have three or more if you can, don't you?"

They talked it over and left themselves open to children right from the honeymoon. In fact, they got pregnant on the honeymoon.

Another couple were thinking of waiting because they were going to move in nine months. After some discussion, however, they decided that early openness to children might be more important than having a comfortable move. They too got pregnant on the honeymoon. Here's what the wife wrote me later:

> Because of our ages we decided to try for a family immediately, and God blessed us: I became pregnant three weeks after the wedding. To the "world" our decision might have seemed foolish. We were newly married, and living on a Navy salary. My husband was planning to leave the Navy in seven months and had no job lined up. However, God's ways are not our ways.
>
> Having a child immediately was the biggest blessing for our marriage. We moved to another state for Eldon's new job when I was 7 ½ months pregnant, and six weeks later Patrick was born. Our new baby brought us closer together right from the start. We focused together on our son, and that helped us bond as a couple. And, having a baby made it easy for us to meet people in our new environment.

And, because we had a child so soon, we never fell into the trap of selfishness with our time or money. So many couples look back wistfully on the time before they had children, when they were free to travel, and to spend more on their pleasures. We never had that period, so we have never missed it.

By having a child right away, we imitated the Holy Family, and the Trinity. What could be more enriching than to turn two into three?

There are any number of reasons couples give for "waiting to have a baby." Some are actually reasons for not getting married yet. Others either ignore the purpose of marriage or the enriching power of having children. I won't go into all the reasons and all the answers here, but let me just urge you to keep in mind these wonderful words from Vatican II, ". . . the very institution of marriage and conjugal love, are ordained to the procreation and education of children and it is in them that they are crowned as by their summit." In other words, the very love of husband and wife tends toward overflowing into children, who ". . . are really the supreme gift of marriage and contribute very much to the good of their parents." How important it is to begin marriage with a full sort of love, a love that is quite willing to generously overflow, bringing forth others to share that love.

This is not to say that natural family planning is wrong, but it should be used only for serious reasons as expressed in *Humanae vitae* and other writings. The point is that when a couple begins married life, they should try to have the full expression of conjugal love which, by definition, includes an openness to life.

Contraception and Natural Family Planning

Another issue you should think about in advance is contraception. The Catholic Church is one of the few institutions to hold out against the wave of contraception which has swept across the world since 1960 when the Pill was introduced. Why is the Church being so "stubborn" as some say?

In a nutshell, here's the story: First, many of the so-called contraceptives, including the IUD, the pill, and Norplant, act as abortifacients either part or all of the time. Abortion is far more serious than contraception, which itself is a serious sin. The barrier methods of contraception are not abortifacients, but their success rate is lower.

What are the moral problems with contraception? Briefly, it impresses an anti-life mentality on the participants.[6] It forms a love which is turned in on the couple, an excluding sort of love. It symbolizes a love which is not total.[7] And, finally it manipulates, and degrades[8] an act which is sacred, and has a delicate harmony designed for the good of the participants.[9]

On the other hand, modern natural family planning (NFP), or natural birth regulation, is 99-plus percent effective, does not depend on a regular cycle, and because it increases communication between husband and wife, those who use it are reported to have a divorce rate of 5 percent or less. Plus, many couples say the abstinence keeps their love fresh, forcing them to concentrate on the other types of love, namely *agape*, friendship and affection. One husband stated it was like having a courtship and honeymoon every month. Need I say more?[10]

How Many Children?

So how many children should a devout Catholic have? They should have as many as they *reasonably* can have. Medical philosopher Dr.

Herb Ratner proposed that the minimum number of children a couple should have for the children's psychological well-being was three and the ideal number, five[11] So, three would be a good minimum number to shoot for, barring serious reasons against it.

What are the reasons to limit children and use natural family planning (NFP)? Pope Paul VI gave some general guidelines in *Humanae vitae*:

> In relation to physical, economic, psychological and social conditions, responsible parenthood is exercised, either by the deliberate and generous decision to raise a numerous family, or by the decision, made for grave motives and with due respect for the moral law, to avoid for the time being, or even for an indeterminate period, a new birth.

Thus if there are serious physical, economic, psychological or social reasons (a *real* population explosion would be a possible social reason) not to have a child, natural family planning can be used to avoid pregnancy.

Can NFP be used to space children? Yes, but the best way to space children is by breast feeding. The ideal spacing for children is said to be about two years. Total breast-feeding, with no supplements and no pacifiers, makes a woman 99 percent infertile for the first six months in the absence of menstruation. After that, the infertility rate drops to 94 percent as solid food is introduced.[12] Thus, if a mother breast feeds her child for a little over a year, the timing of the next child will be ideal.

The benefits of breast-feeding for both mother and child far exceed the benefits of child spacing. And, there are groups ready and indeed, eager, to help women perform this act of love for their children effectively.[13]

Mother at Home

Most data seems to say that children do best with a mother at home. Without doing a doctoral dissertation, here are some of the data I have found:

- "Children who had received the most extensive and earliest childcare (begun during their first year of life) received the poorest teacher and parental ratings for peer relationships, compliance, work habits and emotional health at the age of eight."[14]
- "A large scale synthesis from 88 studies concluded that regular non-parental care for more than 20 hours per week had an unmistakably negative effect on socio-emotional development, behavior and attachment of young children."[15]
- "Ten studies from four different countries related the extended use of daycare to negative and aggressive behavior and decreased cooperation with peers and adults."[16]
- In 2001 *The New York Times* reported on a research project conducted by the National Institute of Child Health and Human Development, a branch of the National Institutes of Health. The *Times* reported that the study "found a direct connection between time spent in child care and traits like aggression, defiance and disobedience . . . [and that] the findings held true regardless of the type or quality of care, the sex of the child, the family's socioeconomic status or whether mothers themselves provided sensitive care." Children nur-

tured by their mothers had one-third the behavior troubles of full-time daycare children.[17]

What if mother has a high-powered career? I've known lawyer and doctor mothers who have stayed home full time with their children. It's a matter of priorities. What will be remembered 50 years from now, your law work or medical work, or the nurturing you gave your young children? And remember, staying home with your young children doesn't mean that you will never be able to have a career again. After they are grown, you can always get back into the job market.

Christian Simplicity

What if the man in the courtship doesn't make enough to have his wife stay home? Bring it up with God. Tell God you'd like to do the best thing for your future children and ask him to help you get a better job so you can do this. And then get to work finding something better *before* you get married and have children.

Sometimes a man makes very little income, but it could be enough for his wife to stay home and raise the children, if the couple would practice real Christian simplicity, as we discussed earlier. In 1991 an article by Brad Lemley appeared in *Parade* magazine about a couple whose income averaged under $30,000 a year for seven years. The wife stayed home to raise her four children and they saved $7,000 a year toward a house. How did they do it? By making every penny count. The wife, Amy Dacyczyn, wrote a book — several, in fact — about how she did it. All of her books include the words, "Tightwad Gazette" in the title and several are still in print.[18]

In another case a working mother who was struggling to balance all her tasks was being interviewed on a TV show. They did an analysis of her income and expenses. When they added it all up, they discovered that if she stayed home she would come out $10 ahead each month. She began to cry. She was trying so hard, and it was all for nothing!

The key to financial security is not to make zillions of dollars, but to be smart about what you do make and to spend it wisely. There are two philosophies of life, as Bishop Fulton J. Sheen used to say. One is to feast first and then suffer the hangover. That is the world's philosophy. The second is to fast first, and then feast. That, of course, is the Christian philosophy.

To apply this to everyday life means that if you live frugally for the first several years of your professional life, never buying anything on credit except your first car and a house, you will be able to live very nicely on what you earn. Why? First, if you begin to buy less, you get into the habit of not spending. You become used to buying only what you really need. Second, you'll save lots of money on interest.

No matter how much money a couple makes, it always seems they need to economize when they marry. You really should start to do that before you marry. When you live simply you are imitating our Blessed Lord. Look how simply he lived. He had very little, to show the world that true riches are not to be found here, but in the life to come. How could a true Christian ever be at peace if he or she were buying luxuries, while others of God's children were without necessities? Helping those in need is necessary for our salvation.

Pope John Paul II wrote in *Familiaris consortio*, "Children must grow up with a correct attitude of freedom with regard to material goods, by adopting a simple and austere lifestyle and being fully convinced that 'man is more precious for what he is than for what he has.' " What better way to teach children a "simple and austere lifestyle" than to live it yourself?

Being careful about money will save you anxiety, arguments with your spouse, and lots of aggravation. It will teach your children not to be materialistic. And if you are generous with the Lord, you'll have all you need in this world, and an abundance in the next.

Education

We need not say much on this, but you should remember that marriage is not ordained just to the procreation of children, but to the procreation *and education* of children. Education is not the responsibility of the state but of the parents.

Vatican II put it beautifully:

> Since parents have given children their life, they are bound by the most serious obligation to educate their offspring and therefore must be recognized as the primary and principal educators. This role in education is so important that only with difficulty can it be supplied where it is lacking. Parents are the ones who must create a family atmosphere animated by love and respect for God and man, in which the well-rounded personal and social education of children is fostered.

Pope John Paul II added to this in *Familiaris consortio*:

> The right and duty of parents to give education is essential, since it is connected with the transmission of human

life; it is original and primary with regard to the educational role of others on account of the uniqueness of the loving relationship between parents and children; and it is irreplaceable and inalienable and therefore incapable of being entirely delegated to others or usurped by others.

Parents are the first educators of their children and they cannot morally give that duty over to the school entirely, be it state-run, or Church-run. They must be the first educators, and they have not only the right, but also the duty to monitor what their children learn in school. If the things their children learn in school are not good, they should either find another school that will teach them the right things, or they should consider home schooling their children.

What About Home Schooling?

While it's not for every one, teaching children at home has become a viable options for many families. Here are some brief facts:

- A nationwide study with a random sample of 1,516 families showed home schoolers averaged 30 percentile points higher on standardized achievement tests than the national average.[19]
- According to a report by the National Home Education Research Institute, Dr. Larry Shyers noted the behavior of children playing and found that the home-educated children had a substantially smaller number of behavioral problems than their conventional-school counterparts. The Institute attributed this to parents being the better behavior models.[20]

- Dr. Raymond S. Moore, former city school superintendent, and university and U. S. Department of Education research officer, says, ". . . the 'rich' socialization privilege of the average school has been proven by many studies instead to guarantee peer dependency, a social cancer in which students lose family closeness and values and provide a precise breeding ground for drugs, ill-advised sex, etc. Many public schools acknowledge this and have sought our [homeschoolers'] help from Alaska and Hawaii to Ohio and Florida."[21]

And, some comments by Dr. Mary Kay Clark:

There is nothing Biblical or remotely Catholic in the idea that children should be placed for at least six hours a day, five days a week, in an environment which continually savages their beliefs. All the secular texts are permeated with anti-Christian values, New Age ideas, feminist views, one-world government or the 'New World Order.' But worst of all . . . with a mentality that everything is relative, that truth is not absolute, that God may not exist, and that every idea is as good as every other.

Socialization is not paganization. I always tell people who ask me about my children's socialization that they are not going to learn bad language, or how to use condoms . . . or how to sneer at sacred things. Our kids will not get socialized if by socialization you mean forming their minds and hearts to take on the same values of the society in which we live. God have mercy on us if we allow our children to be socialized by our essentially pagan society![22]

Summing It Up

Look upon children as a precious gift from God, the "supreme gift of marriage." Be generous in accepting children from the Lord, knowing that, as Julian Simon said, they and the ingenuity they bring, are the greatest resource for the improvement of the world. Try to be open to children early in marriage, to establish a generous, life-giving love from the start. If you need to limit the number of children for serious reasons, use natural family planning. Avoid contraception at all costs.

Be open to having at least three children for a good psychological family atmosphere. Move mountains if necessary, to have a mother at home for her children. Strive to live simply for the love of God. And, take a great interest in the education of your children. Consider homeschooling.

Endnotes

1. All of these elements go to make up what I would call the "personalist" value of having children, something which was often overlooked before Vatican II. Some, alas, were calling having children a "biological end."

2. Julian Simon, who died in 1998, was a senior fellow at the Cato Institute. Fortune Magazine named him one of the 150 Great Minds of the 1990's. He was a graduate of Harvard University, and had a Ph.D. from the University of Chicago Business School. In 1980 Simon offered to bet anyone who would, that any basic commodity (wheat, oil, metals, whatever) would be cheaper ten years later. Population alarmist Paul Erlich made the bet, choosing copper, chrome, nickel, tin and tungsten. Each of them dropped dramatically in price. Erlich had to

pay. Simon's position was that people find, produce and create more resources than they use.

3.   Julian Simon, *The Ultimate Resource II*, Princeton, NJ: Princeton University Press, 1996, p.xxxi.

4.   In the nineties, Danish Statistician Bjorn Lomborg read an article by Simon, in which he asserted that the prophets of doom were wrong. Lomborg became convinced that Simon was just some right-wing propagandist and so he brought together some of his smartest students to prove it. Much to their surprise, they discovered that the facts supported Simon! Lomborg published his research in *The Skeptical Environmentalist: Measuring The Real State of The World*, (Cambridge University Press, 2001).

5.   Peter F. Drucker, *Management Challenges for The 21st Century*, New York: HarperCollins, 1999, p. 44.

6.   This is, of course, a simplification. The theological argument is as follows: The procreative good is always good in itself, it is a basic human good. A contraceptive act goes directly against this good. It is always immoral to act against a basic human good. From Ronald Lawler, OFM Cap., Joseph Boyle, Jr., and William E. May, *Catholic Sexual Ethics*, Huntington, IN: Our Sunday Visitor, 1985, pp. 159ff.

7.   Pope John Paul II, *Familiaris consortio*, n. 32.

8.   *Familiaris consortio*, n. 32.

9.   The most convincing talk ever given on why couples should not contracept is available on tape: "Contraception: Why not?" by Janet Smith. It's available from *One More Soul*, 1-800-307-7685, www.OMSoul.com.

10.   Nona Aguilar received 164 responses to a questionnaire she sent out in the mid-80's to couples of varied educational, social, and religious backgrounds who used natural family plan-

ning. Only one in 164 reported having been divorced and remarried (Nona Aguilar, *The New No-Pill, No-Risk Birth Control*, New York: Rawson, 1986, p. 188). John and Sheila Kippley estimate the divorce rate to be between one in 50 and one in 20, compared to the national average of one in two (John and Sheila Kippley, *The Art of Natural Family Planning*, Cincinnati, OH: Couple to Couple League, 1996, p. 288). These are not comprehensive surveys, and they do not include those who never used any sort of birth control. However, they do indicate that in the US, the divorce rate is much higher for contraceptors, who are in the majority, than for those who use natural family planning.

11. Herbert Ratner, "Cooperate with Nature," a chapter in *Human Life Education*, a book by Anthony Zimmerman. Dr. Ratner, a Jewish convert to the Catholic faith, presented this work in an address to the tenth convention of The Fellowship of Catholic Scholars in 1987. The address can be found at www.ewtn.com/library/FAMILY/NATURE.htm. See page 5.

12. Sheila Kippley, "Summary of Natural Mothering, Breast Feeding and Child Spacing Program," at www.ccli.org/breastfeed/bresfsum.shtml. She says that by making use of natural family planning techniques, the fertility rate, even when solids are being added to the child's diet, can be reduced from 6 percent to 1 percent. Seventy percent of women using her "ecological breast feeding" method had their first menstruation at between 9 and 20 months, with the average being 15 months. See also Sheila Kippley, *Breastfeeding and Natural Child Spacing*, 2nd Edition, Cincinnati, OH: Couple to Couple League, 1989.

13. For example, try La Leche League International at www.lalecheleague.org. They are totally dedicated to helping

women breast feed and overcome the tremendous bias of doctors and others against this healthy practice.

14.   Vandell D.L. & Corasaniti M.A. "Childcare and the Family: Complex contributors to child development" in McCartney. K. *Childcare and Maternal Employment*, San Francisco: Josey-Bass, Inc. 1990. (See www.jbassoc.demon.co.uk/watch/researchdaycare.)

15.   Violata C.& Russell C. "Effects of non-maternal care on child development: a meta-analysis of published research," a paper presented at 55th annual convention of the Canadian Psychological Association. Penticon, British Columbia 1994. (See www.jbassoc.demon.co.uk/watch/researchdaycare.)

16.   Haskins R., "Public School aggression among children with varying daycare experience" *Child Development*, Vol. 56.1985 p 689–703. (See www.jbassoc.demon.co.uk/watch/researchdaycare.)

17.   Sheryl Gay Stolberg, "Link Found Between Behavioral Problems and Time in Child Care," *New York Times*, 19 April 2001. The study began in 1990 and involved over 1,100 children in 10 cities in many different settings. It is considered the most comprehensive child care study to date. (As found in Gregory Flanagan, "Daycare Is Harmful to Children," in *Liberation Journal*, at www.libertocracy.com/Webessays/social/family/daycare/harmful, pp. 2, 3.)

18.   Amy Dacyczyn, *The Complete Tightwad Gazette*, New York: Random House, 1999; and *The Tightwad Gazette: Big Money Saving Guide*, Gramercy Press, 2002.

19.   Ray, Brian D., *A Nationwide Study of Home Education*, Salem, OR: National Home Education Institute, 1990. See Home Education Research Fact Sheet Ic at National Home Education Research Institute web page, www.nheri.org/content.php?menu=1002&page_id=24, p. 1.

20. Larry E. Shyers, "A Comparison of Social Adjustment Between Home and Traditionally Schooled Students," *Home School Researcher*, 8 (3), 1992, pp. 1–8. See Home Education Research Fact Sheet IIb at National Home Education Research Institute web page, www.nheri.org/content.php?menu= 1002&page_id =27, p. 2.

21. Dr. Raymond S. Moore, "Research Shows Benefits of Homeschooling," article found at www.homeeducator.com/HSN/ benefits/htm, p. 2.

22. Mary Kay Clark, *Catholic Home Schooling*, p. 80.

Chapter Sixteen

Christian Engagement

What makes an engagement "Christian"? Some time back a young man shared with me the story of his proposal. It sounded so Christian and so Catholic I obtained his permission to share it. (The names have been changed.)

On February 11th, 2002, Feast of Our Lady of Lourdes, I, Joshua Brown, asked Felicity Smith to be my wife. She said YES!!

This time is so incredibly amazing! The graces of engagement are really powerful and beautiful. God's plan unfolding and strengthening before my eyes is very humbling and awe-inspiring.

Well, about the proposal. I had wanted to ask her on the feast of Our Lady of Lourdes for a while. It is a very special feast to me, and Lourdes is where I once received healing for my knee. It is also simple, quiet, and full of love, and the feast when Mary declared herself as the Immaculate Conception. I didn't know this, and in prayer back in October and November, I kept getting the inspiration that I should ask her on the feast of the Immaculate Conception. Well,

December 8th just didn't sit right. It seemed too rushed. So, I ended up asking her on a feast associated with the Immaculate Conception.

I went and talked to her mom and dad the Tuesday before without Felicity knowing it. I had such joy that morning, since Felicity happened to write me a letter telling me that she was so at peace with our situation and in awe of where the Lord was taking us. Thank you, Jesus. Thank you, Blessed Mother. Thank you, Guardian Angel.

The night before February 11th, I asked Felicity if she would go to the 5:15 Mass with me the next day. We had agreed earlier that week to pray the Novena to Our Lady of Lourdes each day. So, about 5:00 p.m. we go in to 5:15 p.m. Mass in the Crypt Church of the Basilica of the National Shrine of the Immaculate Conception.

After Mass, I asked her to come and pray with me before the tabernacle where there are two kneelers. I had arranged with the security guards ahead of time to clear the place out by the 6:00 p.m. closing time, and give me about 10 minutes to propose. We took a couple minutes to pray. In the meantime, a lady came up about 10 feet away and started praying the Rosary! I thought to myself, "There is no way you are praying that whole Rosary before I get engaged!" So, I motioned to her every way I could to let her know that I was about to propose. She was clueless as to what I was trying to tell her, and actually came closer. Finally I got through to her and she left. Felicity had her head down and didn't really know what was going on.

I then asked Felicity to say a prayer to the Holy Spirit with me for what I was about to do. I then knelt down on both knees and said, "Felicity Elizabeth Cecilia Smith, I now come to you as a man, as a brother, as your best friend, and as a lover. I kneel here before you and before our sweetest Lord Jesus to ask you to be my wife. I invite you on this path to our vocation, so that we can together love and serve God, love and serve each other, and love and serve others. I can't imagine spending the rest of my life without you. Will you marry me?"

She said YES! Yes! Praise God! We held each other for a long time.

Well, there's more. I had placed a Bible and two roses in front of Mary's statue in Our Lady of Lourdes' grotto. I read her the Scripture passage I had picked out, and then we placed roses at the feet of Mary, asking her to be our Mother and guide in these coming months.

Then, I asked her to come with me on a journey. We got in the car, where I played a tape I had made entitled, "45 reasons why Felicity Smith and Joshua Brown should get married." It was both funny and serious.

I drove her to Falls Church, Virginia, where my brother's old roommates have a nice little house with wood floors and a fireplace. My brother prepared a table ahead of time with a picture of Felicity and me from the Easter party we attended in Steubenville right after we started dating. We had wine, candles, a fire in the fireplace, and food from Maggiano's, our favorite Italian restaurant. It was a fun intimate time for both of us. Of course, I sang her the John Denver song Follow Me. Then, the three roommates came in with Mexican sombreros and serenaded us.

Finally, we went back to her apartment and found my brother, her sister Jen, and Emily. Little did we know, they had prepared the whole room with candles and pictures of us, and had made fondue and champagne. After some delightful conversation and affirmation, they prayed over us.

What a beautiful night! It is amazing how when we surrender to God's holy will, he allows things to go so very smoothly and peacefully. But, every grace is preceded by a time of trial and abandonment. I see clearly how in any big decision we make, we will usually not receive consolation, but only a deep abiding knowledge in our hearts from prayer.

Praise God!! I am so happy and so blessed to be so in love with such a woman, who reflects for me the beauty of God in everything she is and does. A heartfelt "Thank you" to you all for your role in making Felicity and me who we are, through your prayers, love, friendship, words, actions, and presence. I love you all.

Speaking to Her Father

As Joshua so dutifully did, it is customary among the devout and the polite, for the man to ask permission from his sweetheart's father to propose to his daughter. It's delightfully old-fashioned; one of those traditions that so symbolizes family unity. Amidst the disarray of what our culture has made of courtship, this custom is coming back. Thanks be to God.

Must this always be done? No, not if there are serious reasons against it: for instance, the father finds her sweetheart "too darned religious," and has his mind set on having his daughter marry a rich nonbeliever instead. But if things are right, this is a noble way to proceed.

Engagement Courtship

Once you get engaged, you need to see each other more often, right? No. There is no need to get overly clingy once you get engaged. If you have been seeing each other two or three times a week, that should be fine for engagement as well. It may be that some weeks you'll have to do more things together as you prepare for the wedding, but you shouldn't feel obliged to smother each other with your presence just because you are engaged. Just keep up the same pattern. One note of caution, however. Just because you see each other for preparation activities, does not mean you can drop off the courtship activities. You still need to go out to dinner or go dancing periodically during the engagement time. Dating is an important thing even for married couples. That intimate time together is very important at any stage in a relationship.

Contact a Priest

Once he has proposed and she has said yes, it is time to speak to a priest about having the wedding. Ordinarily, parishes require at least a six-month preparation time for a wedding, but most couples allow much more than that — a year or more. Once you have decided to marry, that's the time to see the priest. Even if you don't have a date in mind, he may be able to help you decide on a good time to get married.

To which parish should you go, his or hers? Traditionally, weddings are held in the bride's parish, but you may have the wedding in either. Or, if you wish to marry in another parish for a good reason, you may do so by getting the permission of your own pastor, and of course, the approval of the parish where you want to marry.

In any event, the bride should have the primary say as to where the wedding takes place — not the groom, and not the bride's mother or father, although she ought to consider their input, especially the groom's. She should try to choose the church where she attends Mass ordinarily. If she has only recently moved from her home town, she could have the wedding back there if the home town pastor is willing. In any event, she should decide on the church with the agreement of the groom, keeping in mind the convenience of the most number of people. And, she should choose the reception site with the same criteria in mind.

What if you have a good priest friend whom you would like to officiate at your wedding? This is ordinarily no problem, presuming the priest is in good standing. Simply ask the priest if he would be willing to do the ceremony, and then ask the parish priest if you may have a visiting priest officiate.

Some parishes are so popular that you need to reserve a time a year or more in advance. Once you have a date in mind, and you have already spoken to the priest and done some preliminaries with him, that's the time for the priest to see what times are available for the wedding on that date and for the rehearsal as well. You may have to change the date to get the time you want. This is why it is important to arrange the date and time with the church first, before you even think of a reception place.

Those that book the reception first, and then go to the church, in addition to betraying an infelicitous set of priorities, may find themselves having to pay a fee to change the reception date because the church is not available.

Marriage Preparation

Marriage preparation is ordinarily done in the parish where you plan to marry, but for a good reason, it may be done by any priest. I once did the marriage preparation for a couple who was to be married in a neighboring parish, by the bride's brother, who was a priest in another parish. The couple thought it was best to do their preparation with a priest other than the bride's brother, who was the obvious choice to do the wedding.

Generally, there are several elements to marriage preparation in the Church:

1. The initial interview with the priest.
2. The "prenuptial investigation" (PNI) — a standard questionnaire which is filled out by the priest with the couple.
3. Some sort of pre-marital inventory (PMI). There are several of these in use, such as FOCUSS and Prepare/Enrich. If your priest does not ordinarily use one, ask to take one. They are *very* worthwhile. They involve a large number of questions dealing with a wide range of issues which could affect your marriage. Ordinarily you take the "test" and then after it is processed by a computer, you discuss the results with the priest. It will often uncover areas you may not have discussed yet, and at times it has revealed problems serious enough that the couple has decided not to marry.
4. Marriage Preparation Classes which may be in the form of a series of classes (usually a half-dozen or fewer) with a priest and some married couples. Or, you may take an "Engaged Encounter" weekend. The latter, since it involves staying at a hotel or retreat center, costs more. These classes are very important. Not all of them are good, however. So, you should

ask around among solidly Catholic priests and other friends
to find out which of these are the best.

5. Some of the paperwork ordinarily required is a new baptismal certificate for the Catholic party(s). This should be dated
within six months of the wedding. If there is some difficulty
getting a baptismal certificate (for example, if the church
where a person was baptized was destroyed) a letter from
someone who has known the person all his life stating he/
she has never been married could be accepted instead. In
some places such a letter is required even if the baptismal
certificate is received.

6. A dispensation is required if the Catholic is marrying an un-
baptized person. Permission from the Bishop's office is required for a Catholic to marry a baptized non-Catholic. The
same form can ordinarily be used for either. It requires that
the Catholic sign a statement to the effect that he/she will
continue to live the Catholic faith and do all in his/her power
to raise the children Catholic.[1] The non-Catholic party
should be aware of this requirement and verbally agree to it.

7. A marriage license must be obtained from the state in the
county where the wedding is to take place. Generally the
license is only good for a fixed time, for example, sixty days.
In some states you must both get a blood test to get a marriage license.

Bachelor Party

The traditional bachelor party over the past fifty or so years has
been anything but Christian. In many cases it has been a farewell
to the freedoms of the bachelor, analogous to the "farewell to the

flesh," the "Carnival" practiced in Brazil, Italy, and other countries on Mardi Gras, the Tuesday before Ash Wednesday. Both are a pagan lament over the commitment involved in either marriage or the Lenten practices of self-denial. Both focus on the negative aspects of two very noble things.

Granted, there is a certain degree of facetiousness in all of this, but things are often carried beyond what is in keeping with human dignity. At some bachelor parties there is too much drinking, and even a denigration of marriage and sex.

The priest who taught me the theology of marriage suggested that it would be more apt to have a retreat before a wedding than a bachelor party. Perhaps our retreat centers might arrange for one or two weekends each year for marriage preparation retreats for men, and some for women as well.

Nevertheless, it wouldn't hurt for the guys to get together and have what might be called a Christian bachelor party if they like. I attended one at which the groom was roasted in a good clean fashion. If the men hold a roast, it might be a nice touch to invite each roaster to read at the end a short quote about the goodness of marriage, or to make up a nice toast, praising the couple and the state of marriage.

The Final Week

More than once, a bride has called me less than a week before the wedding and said something like, "Father, I don't know if I can marry this man. He is acting like such a jerk!" And these are good Catholic couples!

The week before a wedding can be the most stressful time in anyone's life. When people are stressed they can say the darnedest things. This is not a time to panic. I always tell the bride — and groom — not to worry so much about arguments in that final week. If the previous three months have been good, and he or she doesn't do anything bizarre like having an affair with a member of the wedding party, go ahead with the wedding. These last-minute fallouts are fairly common. Perhaps that's why there is a superstition about not seeing each other on the morning of the wedding. When these crises come up I always tell the bride, "What you're feeling is fairly common. Stay away from him until the wedding."

I would recommend to all couples that they don't try to see too much of each other the week before the wedding. Absence, especially in that final week, will surely make the heart grow fonder.

Summing It Up

For a truly Christian engagement, try to propose in a religious setting, and pray together in gratitude for the Lord's bringing you together. The man should ask permission of the woman's father before proposing. Don't try to see each other any more often once you are engaged, but don't forget to have some fun dates even if you are seeing each other a good deal to work out wedding plans. Take marriage preparation seriously, and enthusiastically fulfill all the requirements. They are for your own good. For a Christian bachelor party, the groom should tell his friend organizing it, that he wants little drinking, no impurity, and for each one to say something positive about marriage, even if they have a roast. And don't worry too much about flare-ups during the final week. If the previous three months have gone well, then forge ahead with the wedding.

Endnotes

1. Why is this required? Because if we believe that the Catholic faith was established by Jesus Christ, God himself, and is sustained by him (see Matthew 28:20), as indeed we do, we have a moral obligation to raise our children in that faith.

Chapter Seventeen

A Catholic Wedding

How seldom it is that we priests have the opportunity to officiate at a truly Catholic wedding, the kind of wedding that Mary or some of the saints would have if they were marrying today. In fairness, it's not always the fault of the bride and groom. Some have never gotten good advice as to how to have a wedding that would please the Lord.

Modest Dresses

A bride who is trying to please the Lord more than the world will think carefully about her dress and those of her bride's maids as well. A truly modest bride's dress will have sleeves (short for a warm-weather wedding, long for cooler weather), and a neckline that covers the breasts completely. The back neckline should be fairly high as well. The bride's maids' dresses should reflect a similar design. One bride's maid even remarked to me at the rehearsal dinner about the dresses they were supposed to wear, "I don't feel comfortable dressing that way in church." Priests don't always remember to speak about dress in the first couple of meetings. And, if they wait, it is often too late. So here's an early heads up to the brides: dress for Christ, not for the world.

The Priest

Certainly if you want a really Catholic wedding you should choose a holy priest. Generally, it will have to be one of the priests in the parish where you marry, unless you know another priest well. So if you don't have a personal relationship with one of the priests, ask the one who prays a lot, who loves the Mass, the Eucharist, the Blessed Mother, and the Church.

Nuptial Mass

Because of the tremendous graces you receive from the Mass, I strongly recommend you have a nuptial Mass for your wedding. This would be natural if both bride and groom are Catholic. Some priests discourage a Mass if a person is marrying a non-Catholic (if you marry a non-Christian you may not have a Mass), since it will be somewhat divisive in that at least a portion of the congregation will not be able to receive Communion. As true as that may be, the grace received from a Nuptial Mass should far outweigh any incon-venience caused by the differences in religion.

I announce at every wedding at Communion time, "Those Catholics who are living in the state of grace and attending Mass every Sunday are welcome to come up to receive Communion af-ter the wedding party. Those who are not in that category, are wel-come to come up and receive a blessing." Non-Catholics and non-practicing Catholics seem quite satisfied with this arrangement.

Mass Readings and More

Generally the priest will give you a small booklet or handout con-taining a list of recommended wedding readings. You may choose other Biblical readings if you like, but the ones recommended by the Church are usually well-suited to a wedding. I would propose the following as my own favorites:

First Reading: Genesis 2:18–24 (Speaks of God's creation of woman and the man leaving his father and mother and clinging to his wife.)

Responsorial Psalm: Psalm 128:1–5 (The response is "Happy are they who fear the Lord" and the Psalm speaks of how blessed one will be in his work, his wife and children if he does fear the Lord.)

Second Reading: 1 Corinthians 12:31–13:8 (This is *very* popular because it is very apt. Paul speaks of the virtues in love: "Love is patient, love is kind, love is not jealous. . . .")

Gospel: Matthew 22:35–40 (The two great commandments of love); or

Mark 10:6–9 (Jesus quotes Genesis as above, and ends with "What God has joined together, man must not divide.")

You should check with the priest on the gospel. He may want to choose it himself since it should fit with his homily. You may also have the option of choosing the opening and closing prayers, the preface, the nuptial blessing, and so on. I recommend you leave these things to the priest because, (a) It's a lot of work for you to choose them and (b) It's very hard for the priest to keep track of each choice, and he may forget what you've chosen.

You also have the option of choosing as many as four readers for the following: (1) First reading; (2) Responsorial Psalm (but I recommend you have the cantor sing this); (3) Second reading; and (4) the Intercessory Prayers. If you have a nuptial Mass, the readers must be Catholic. I strongly suggest that you only choose people who have been trained to be lectors at Mass, or at least who know how to do public reading well. If you don't know anyone who has experience reading, you may have the priest do all the readings.

You may compose the intercessory prayers yourself, if you like. Few couples do that. In fact, most couples have the priest lead the intercessions. However, it is quite nice for you to make a list of your deceased relatives and include a prayer for them in the intercessions.

Vows

You should choose your vows, however. These are the vows I would recommend:

> I, _____, take you _____, to be my (husband or wife). I promise to be true to you in good times and in bad, in sickness, and in health. I will love you and honor you all the days of my life.

Usually the priest will lead you through these vows by saying them, and having you repeat his words. You may, of course, memorize your vows, if you want to live dangerously. The only couple I can remember who ever did this came to the time for the vows and the groom said, "I Herbert, take you Penelope, to be my husband . . ." I interrupted, "Wife! wife! . . ."

Music

Having good, religious music is crucial for a bone fide Catholic wedding. The first rule for a Church wedding is to have sacred music, music which is focused on God. Ordinarily you will make an appointment to meet with the music director of your parish and go over the possible music selections for the wedding. This should take place at least three months before the big day. Here are some suggestions of sacred music used at weddings:

Prelude: Pie Jesu; Jesu, Joy of Man's Desiring

Processional: Rigadoun by Andre Campra, and Trumpet Voluntary by Jeremiah Clarke (Often there are two processionals, one for the wedding party and another for the bride.)

Offertory Hymn: Holy Is His Name by John Michael Talbot (contemporary)

Communion Hymn: Panis Angelicus; Ave Verum Corpus

Hymn During Prayer to Mary: Ave Maria by Charles Gounod

Recessional: Horn Pipe from Water Music Suite No. 2 (Handel)

Postludes: Alleluia from Exsultate, Jubilate (Mozart); Allegro from Trumpet Concerto in A Flat (Vivaldi); Praise Be to God, Cantata No. 129 (Bach); Andante Allegro from Water Music Suite No. 2 (Handel) (I strongly encourage that you use postludes to cover the noise after the ceremony.)

If you want a music preview before you meet with the music director, you can hear many of these by going to www.buy.com or www.amazon.com or some other music vendor on the web and type in wedding music. Click on one of the CD's which has classical music and then click on the music piece to hear it.

Additionally, I recommend that you ask for both an organist and a cantor as a minimum.

The Wedding Program

Although programs are not necessary for a wedding, they are sometimes useful, especially if many non-Catholics will be attending. Most priests or music directors can show you sample programs of previous weddings. (See Appendix.)

If you know how to do desktop publishing you can compose it on your computer and then print it out camera-ready to give to the printer. The usual size is 8 ½ x 11, folded in two to make a booklet 8 ½ x 5 ½. You may use one sheet, or two, depending on how much information you include. Of course you should try to find a nice heavy weight ivory or other fancy paper. Generally printers will be able to make some good suggestions regarding paper. If you want the programs by Friday, give the printer a Tuesday deadline.

The Rehearsal

The rehearsal should generally be the evening before the wedding, and should take into account the fact that many in the wedding party may be coming after work. A popular time for the rehearsal is at 6:00 or 6:30 p.m. on Friday for a Saturday wedding. This way people can come after work, but there is still time for the rehearsal dinner. And remember, people should dress nicely for the rehearsal. After one rehearsal and dinner, we had a Eucharistic holy hour at the church. That was impressive!

If you want the priest to get to know you and the wedding party better, you may invite him to the rehearsal dinner. Many priests are more likely to attend the rehearsal than the reception, since Friday nights are far easier to get away from the parish than Saturday afternoons. If you invite the priest to the rehearsal dinner, be sure to invite him at the same time you send out your invitations or six weeks before the wedding, whichever is earlier.

When you meet with the priest to speak about the rehearsal, you might ask if he will be able to offer confessions after the rehearsal. Many priests do that as a matter of course, but not all. The bride and groom should be the first in the confessional, not only because this is a great thing to do before your wedding, but also to set a good example for the others. Offering confession after the rehearsal is one more element of a "truly Catholic wedding," and sometimes these confessions are very worthwhile.

Traditional Wedding Format

Ordinarily a priest will have a format which he follows for weddings, and he will allow the bride and groom to propose any (reasonable) changes to that format. I will propose here a traditional wedding format so that you will have a baseline to work from. First, the groom and the best man go to the sacristy a half-hour before the wedding time to wait with the priest. The other groomsmen/ushers are at the door by that same time to usher guests into the church. Unless there are far more guests for the bride than the groom, or vice versa, the ushers should ask the guest, "Are you a guest of the bride or groom?" and then, depending on their answer, seat them on the bride's (left) or groom's (right) side of the church as they enter.

The bride should arrive fifteen minutes before the wedding begins, along with the rest of the wedding party, and the parents of both bride and groom. When the ladies are ready, they tell one of the groomsmen and the latter escorts the groom's parents to the second pew on the right. Then a groomsman escorts the mother of the bride to the second pew on the left. After that they inform the organist and the priest that all are ready to begin.

The music begins and the bride's maids enter one by one, with half the length of the aisle separating them. The bride should determine the order in which they enter, based on size or on how close their ties with the bride are. One of the things that marks a truly Catholic wedding is for each of the bride's maids to genuflect before the tabernacle when she gets to the front of the church. After they genuflect, the bride's maids would enter the first pew, one by one. I always try to put the wedding party in the first pew, even in churches where there are several chairs or benches up on the altar, because all those people can be a great distraction during the ceremony and Mass, especially when they are ill-behaved, which is often the case.

The priest comes out to the altar, and the best man and the groom (in that order) walk out in front of the first pew and wait for the maid of honor and the bride to come down the aisle. When the maid of honor arrives, the best man offers his elbow and escorts her up to the altar, where they split off and go to their respective places. The flower girl and ring bearer (if any) would follow here in the procession and go into the pew with their parents.

The bride is escorted down the aisle by her father, and when they get to the front he will usually lift her veil, kiss her on the cheek, and hand her over to the groom. The groom then escorts her up to the altar and they stand before their kneeler as the priest begins the Mass.

After the gospel the priest comes forward and all stand. He invites the wedding party to come and stand next to the bride and groom strung out in a kind of line or semicircle, with the maid of honor and best man closest to the bride and groom respectively. By having the bridal party come forth at this time and at the closing, attention is drawn to these two important moments of the wedding.

Generally, the bride and groom will face the priest and the altar behind him as they prepare to exchange their vows. This is certainly the traditional way, and the most theologically sound, because it emphasizes that the wedding is a prayer and promise before God, not a show for the congregation. When the vows are actually exchanged, the bride and groom face each other. Once the vows are exchanged and the rings are blessed and exchanged, all go back to their places. The marriage commitment is made.

The priest continues with the Eucharistic prayer, the Our Father, and the nuptial blessing. After that comes Communion. After Communion, the bride and groom generally will kneel in thanksgiving for their having received two sacraments, Matrimony and the Eucharist. Once Holy Communion is completed, the priest comes down and invites the wedding party up to the sanctuary again. Then he says the closing prayer.

At that point, the bride may bring a bouquet of flowers over to the statue of the Blessed Virgin Mary and kneel for a few minutes in prayer, asking Mary to help her to be a good wife and mother. (This is *very* Catholic.) Generally, the groom will accompany her there and stand while she kneels before Mary's statue. During this time the cantor will usually sing the Ave Maria. The couple should time their visit to Mary so that they return while the music is still being sung.

Then the priest gives the final blessing. If the couple wishes, the priest may say, "I now present to you Mr. and Mrs. John Kelly," at which point the congregation will probably applaud. Then the priest will usually say to the groom, "You may kiss the bride." At this point, the groom should slowly and tenderly kiss his bride on the lips and perhaps, give her a nice slow hug. Following this, the music begins, and the bride and groom lead the wedding party down the aisle.

If they intend to have pictures after the wedding, the bridal party must continue across the back of the church and down a side aisle back to the altar. This is so as to avoid a receiving line at the church which can take half an hour or more.

Irreverences to Avoid

There are a number of things you need to beware of as a couple that can make your wedding decidedly *not* Catholic. The first is misbehavior on the altar (i.e., in the sanctuary). At one wedding two "Maids of Honor" were on the altar, facing the congregation. They chatted during half the ceremony. During the homily, one of them was signaling to the bride who was signaling back. At one point I had had enough. I stopped, looked at the bride, smiled and put my finger up to my lips. She got the message. The pastor, who was concelebrating was livid. Everyone sees irreverent behavior in the sanctuary, and it is very distracting.

In general, it's good to urge the wedding party one by one to be on their best, and most reverent behavior during the ceremony. A wedding Mass is a sacred event, not a rock concert. It never hurts to ask the priest to announce at the rehearsal the need for attention and reverence during the ceremony.

Another thing that can ruin a wedding is a pushy photographer. I had just such a photographer at a wedding at the Cathedral in Washington. When he showed up in army fatigues I knew he was going to be trouble. As the bride entered, he kept having her stop so he could get some good shots. Then he kept moving around in front of the congregation, distracting everyone. Finally, I asked the best man to go down and tell him to stay in one place and not to block the view of the congregation. When he didn't reform, I threatened to ask him to leave.

Another photographer showed up in the middle of the wedding in the sanctuary, behind the altar. I stopped, and pointed my finger for him to leave immediately. A photographer should never be in the sanctuary, and if there is videotaping, the one doing it should not distract people by moving his light all around the church. The point is, be sure to get a photographer who is sensitive to the sacredness of the event. A wedding is a sacred event, not a "photo op."

Be Ready for Glitches

One thing every bride and groom should realize is that no matter how well you plan a wedding, something will always go differently than you planned; some strange thing will happen. Once I had to wake up the best man as the maid of honor walked right by him and into the sanctuary. Another time, a priest told me the bride fainted at her wedding. Another priest couldn't remember the name of the groom during the ceremony. And, it was his own brother!

The key is to be prepared for the unexpected. Sometimes the couple will forget the marriage license. A priest is not legally permitted to marry a couple that does not have a marriage license. Bring the license to the rehearsal and give it to the priest then.

Be sure to contact the priest who is doing your wedding during that final week before the event. One priest (who eventually became a bishop), told the story of the day he totally forgot about a wedding he was supposed to witness. He was returning from lunch an hour or two after the wedding time when he saw the bride out in front of the church. His jaw dropped about a foot. He went in and witnessed the wedding, but the day was not a happy one for the couple (or the priest). At another wedding I had, the groom couldn't find the ring and one of the married men lent him his own ring.

At another wedding the priest was kidding the groom in the sacristy. "Now, if you change your mind about this wedding, you can go out the back door here, and cross the field there and you're gone." When he came out to the altar the congregation was laughing. He couldn't figure out why, until someone told him, "Father, you had your mike on in there. Everyone heard you!"

Brides (and grooms), not to worry. Know that something goes wrong at just about every wedding. Don't obsess. Most often the priest will be able to get you through it nicely, and in many cases not a single guest will notice. Do your best to plan, and then leave the rest up to the Lord.

Think Simple!

Weddings can sometimes be a great challenge to those trying to live Christian simplicity. We generally think of a wedding as the time when we pull out all the stops. But sometimes that can go much too far, especially at the reception.

I've officiated at scores of weddings, and the receptions which were most pleasant and impressive were not the most expensive ones at fancy hotels, but the most creative ones. Two of my nieces had their receptions at country clubs. In general, these are less expensive than hotels. For another niece's wedding, her parents put up a big tent in their back yard and the reception was held there.

One bride had a friend who offered her lovely big house for the reception. It was elegant, but I suspect, not as expensive as a hotel reception. Some of the nicest receptions I have attended have been in parish halls, nicely furnished for wedding receptions. Some Knights of Columbus or VFW halls are very worthy places for wedding receptions. One couple had their reception at a mansion which often hosts social events in Washington. Another rented a garden restaurant for an afternoon when they would ordinarily be closed.

Recently, a nice young couple from New York told me they were planning to have their wedding at the Church of Our Savior on Park Avenue and then have a potluck dinner for their reception in the parish hall downstairs. Some friends of the groom told him they were glad he did that because it took the pressure off for their own receptions. The point is, if we are really Christian, we should strive to do things nicely, but not garishly expensive. Think hospitality, think good food and wine, but think moderate as well. A little creativity in finding a place can bring that about.

Before we move on from receptions, here's a delightful thing I saw at one reception. The couple had someone announce that the newlyweds will not be kissing for ringing glasses, but only in response to a song by one of the guests which mentions the word "love." Each table came up with a song, and then one or more people stood and sang their piece. What fun!

As for other customs, forget the throwing of the bride's garter at the reception, please. And you need not go to the expense of having a live band at the reception. A DJ works fine and is much more economical.

Another thing to consider is not overdoing the number of people in the wedding party. Three or four bride's maids and the same number of groomsmen should be enough.

Creativity can be applied to the rehearsal dinner as well as the reception. Since the numbers for this are generally small, a dinner at home is often possible. I've been to several nice rehearsal dinners in people's homes.

Limousines are another expense. One creative couple rented a Lincoln Town Car and had a friend drive them around in it. What a great wedding present that would be from one of the groom's buddies. (Buy him a nice chauffeur's hat!)

Flowers can get very expensive. If you get married within a week of Christmas or Easter, you may not need any more flowers. The place will be covered with them. Some parishes help brides getting married on the same day to coordinate their flower purchases so that they can use the same flowers for both weddings.

The point of all this is, that as Christians, we should try to do things nicely, with taste, by being as hospitable as possible, without spending a ton of money. The money you save can go to the poor or the Church.

Summing It Up

To have a Catholic wedding, begin with modest dresses. Ask the holiest priest available to do the wedding, and have a nuptial Mass. Choose experienced readers and good religious music. Ask participants to dress nicely for the rehearsal and ask the priest to hear confessions right after the rehearsal. Have a general idea of how the wedding will take place, and politely ask for any (reasonable) variations from what the priest proposes. Choose bridesmaids and groomsmen who will not embarrass you at the altar, and a photographer who will be respectful and reverent in church. Remember, no matter how well you plan the wedding, something, usually some little thing, will go wrong. Don't give it a second thought. And, finally, try to have a nice reception, but exercise Christian moderation. A wedding is big, but pleasing God is bigger.

Appendix

Sample Wedding Program

If you would like to download this wedding program from the web, so as to avoid having to retype it, go to www.cfalive.org and click on "Wedding Program." You may find the wedding readings which can be included in your wedding program without obtaining permission at www.setonscene.org/Parish_Info/wedding_readings.htm.

The Nuptial Mass Uniting

Esmeralda Perpetua McGillicutty

And

Horatio Melvin Benedetti

In

The Sacrament of Holy Matrimony

಄

August 5, 2008

St. Teresa's Catholic Church

New Towne, Maryland

Celebrant

Reverend Sean O'Donnell

Concelebrants

Reverend John Smith
Reverend Alberto Rivas

Parents of the Bride

Mr. and Mrs. Mortimer McGillicutty

Parents of the Groom

Mr. and Mrs. Alfio Benedetti

The Wedding Party

Maid of Honor
Mary-Ann McGillicutty .... *Sister of the Bride*

Best Man
David Benedetti .... *Brother of the Groom*

Bridesmaids
Elvira Patterson .... *Friend of the Bride*
Melanie Brown .... *Friend of the Bride*
Suzanne McGillicutty .... *Sister of the Bride*

Groomsmen
Peter O'Brien .... *Friend of the Groom*
Rolf Mancuso .... *Friend of the Groom*
Brendan Devlin .... *Friend of the Groom*

Flower Girl
Melissa McGillicutty .... *Niece of the Bride*

Ring Bearer
Ambrose Milano .... *Nephew of the Bride*

Lectors
Imogene Pierce .... *Friend of the Bride*
Marla Adams .... *Sister of the Bride*
Desmond Toomey .... *Nephew of the Groom*

Musicians
Vocalist: Brenda Morrison
Organist: Martha Wellstone

Musical Selections
Preludes
Ave Maria .... Franz Schubert
Pie Jesu .... Andrew Lloyd Webber
Jesu Joy of Man's Desiring .... Johann Sebastian Bach

Processionals
Adagio .... A. Vivaldi
Rigadoun .... Andre Campra
Trumpet Voluntary .... Jeremiah Clark

At the commencement of the Trumpet Voluntary, please stand.

Introductory Rites

Greeting

Penitential Rite

Opening Prayer

Liturgy of the Word

First Reading .... Imogene Pierce
Genesis 2: 18–24
[Permission would be needed from copyright holder to include Scripture text here.]

Responsorial Psalm .... Marla Adams
Psalm 128:1–5
Response: Happy are they who fear the Lord.

Second Reading .... Desmond Toomey
Colossians 3:12–17
Alleluia (Please stand.)

Gospel .... Rev. John Smith
John 15: 12–16
All Respond: Praise to you, Lord Jesus Christ.

Homily (Please be seated.)... Rev. Sean O'Donnell

Rite of Marriage

Exchange of Vows

Blessing and Exchange of Rings

Prayer of the Faithful
Marvin Bello

Liturgy of the Eucharist

Preparation of the Gifts
Presentation of the Gifts
Mortimer and Felicity McGillicutty (Parents of the Bride)
Alfio and Margot Benedetti (Parents of the Groom)
Pray, Brethren
(Please stand when the priest begins, "Pray, brethren, that our sacrifice may be acceptable. . . .")
Prayer Over the Gifts

Eucharistic Prayer
(Please kneel.)

Lord's Prayer
(Please stand.)

Nuptial Blessing

Sign of Peace

Communion Rite

(All Catholics who are regularly attending Mass and are in the state of grace are welcome to come forward to receive Communion.)

Concluding Rite

Closing Prayer

Dedication to Mary

Ave Maria .... Charles Gounod

Final Blessing and Dismissal

Recessional

Horn Pipe .... G. F. Handel

Postludes

Alleluia from Exsultate, Jubilate .... W. A. Mozart

Allegro from Trumpet Concerto in A Flat .... A. Vivaldi

Praise Be to God, Cantata No. 129 .... J. S. Bach

Andante Allegro from Water Music Suite No. 2 ... G. F. Handel

Postscript

Thank you kindly for reading this book. I sincerely hope it will help you to find a life-long spouse who will help you get to God's Kingdom. Please, if you have any positive suggestions for improvement, or you have stories of how some of the suggestions herein have helped you, do email me at frmorrow@mindspring.com. I would like very much to hear from you.

About the Author

Father T. G. Morrow worked for twelve years as an engineer before entering seminary and being ordained a priest for the Archdiocese of Washington in 1982. He was host for three years (1989-1992) of **Catholic Faith Alive!**, a radio program in which he explained the Catholic Faith. He is co-founder of the St. Catherine Society and St. Lawrence Society for single women and men respectively, which now have chapters in Maryland, Washington, DC, New York, and Virginia. Fr. Morrow has an STL in Moral Theology from the Dominican House of Studies and a doctorate in Sacred Theology from the Pope John Paul II Institute for Studies on Marriage and Family. His other writing can be found at www.cfalive.org.

See the newest titles online or ask for a catalog.

OurSundayVisitor

Bringing Your Catholic Faith to Life

www.osv.com

1-800-348-2440 x3

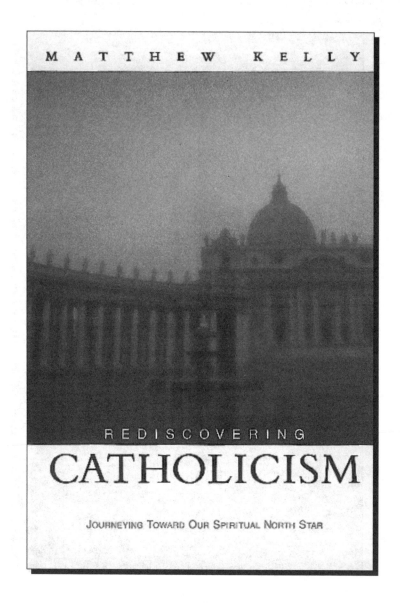